Management Science in Business

By Stanley J. PoKempner

*A Research Report from The Conference Board's
Division of Management Research
Harold Stieglitz, Vice President*

About This Report

This study examines the status of the practice of management science units in business. It describes management science unit projects, under what circumstances these units operate, and how they approach their problems. At the least, it conveys a sense of the range and type of management problems with which management scientists cope in business. At best, it will serve those executives wishing to understand the strengths and weaknesses of a valuable resource – a resource that they may want to use in their decision making. The study is based upon information gleaned mainly from a two-phase research study in which 492 industrial and service firms and 296 managers of units doing management science work took part.

Part One of the report examines the origins and functions of management science in business. In addition to the age and originating circumstances of units, this section dis-

cusses the compensation and educational background of management scientists and provides an informative review of how they view their profession's strengths and weaknesses. There is also a report of the frequency, the contribution, and the effort associated with a broad range of MS projects in the major functional areas of business.

Part Two deals with the management scientist within the context of the corporate organization. The incidence and setting of the units, as well as the administrative issues affecting MS practice, are reviewed. Finally, management scientists express preferences and thoughts about their profession's future.

Appendixes contain supplemental statistical tables, measures of the usage of management science tools, and a glossary, as well as a comprehensive description of the survey and the case studies of MS units in five major companies.

Contents

Tables

Charts

Exhibits

Appendixes

Foreword

MANAGEMENT SCIENTISTS, whatever their titles, are demonstrating their ability to adapt the analytical tools of contemporary mathematics to the world of business. They are helping to solve problems that range from those troubling chief executives to those affecting management on the factory floor. Their disciplines find use in the clarification of strategic questions as well as in the untangling of the intricacies of business logistics.

Business executives are exploiting the fruits of the combination of scientific analysis and pragmatic expertise that evolved from the military operations-research groups of World War II. Whether performed by professionals in formal business units that practice management science/operations research exclusively, or performed by other units doing identical problem-solving services under a variety of titles, this specialized support function is active across the spectrum of business decision making.

The unremitting pace of new technology, as well as the novel complexities that arise, may crystallize a unique business domain for the management science professionals. In its incipient form, however, this domain is not easy to describe, simple to define, or even obvious as a common functional form in business.

It is the kinds of problems and the variety of business areas in which management scientists work – as well as the projects to which they apply their specialized skills – that ultimately identify their domain and the measure of their functional value. To further the more effective use by management of this analytical resource, its domain has been studied by The Conference Board across a wide spectrum of business firms and the management science units they identified. The findings of this study and selected case studies comprise the bulk of this report.

The research and resulting report were produced by Stanley J. PoKempner, senior research associate for management sciences and information systems, under the general direction of James K. Brown, director, management systems and planning research.

The Board is grateful to the firms and managers of units identified as doing management science work that contributed to this study, and especially to the five companies whose case studies are included in the final section of the report. The Board also acknowledges with appreciation the contribution of a number of leading academic and practicing management scientists whose suggestions helped formulate the research design.

KENNETH A. RANDALL
President

Author's Acknowledgments

Special credits are due to Michael Papantoniou for his professional skills in handling the statistical and data processing aspects of the study; to Margaret E. Baxter for her assistance in preparing statistical tables for publication, and to Joan Mastriocovo and Gloria Augustine for their care in preparing the manuscript for publication.

Especial acknowledgment is due Richard J. Jupa for his skillful and patient editorial shepherding of the manuscript to production.

Part One
Management Science: Its Origins and Functions

Chapter 1
Introduction

BUSINESSMEN have always felt at home dealing with numbers, but their actual acceptance of mathematical analysis has come harder and occurred only in the last few decades. Management science (or its synonym, operations research) is the application of mathematical analysis to the systematic study of managerial systems, and is among the more recent of a number of attempts to bring science to business.[1] These attempts began with the scientific management movement initiated at the turn of the century by Frederick W. Taylor to introduce the methods and language of science into the practice of management.

Management science grew out of the experience of scientific specialists in operations research (or, in Great Britain, operational research) groups in World War II. With woefully inadequate resources, these groups developed means to implement the new technology of radar in defending Britain from enemy aircraft. They also provided systematic antisubmarine procedures for stanching the loss of shipping, again with minimal use of scarce resources; and they established the bases for effective management of the vast flows of logistical support for the global war effort. Their success led some businesses to adopt their approach and techniques in the immediate postwar years.

But even with the management scientists' tools vastly enhanced by the advent of the computer, their penetration into industry was slow. In part, the difficulty of transferring procedures for the achievement of easily identified military objectives to the more flexible, more volatile business environment explains this lag. Also, the communications gap between mathematically trained MS practitioners and rigidly pragmatic business managers inhibited a wider acceptance. Indeed, for a period, it seemed that MS might become another passing fad.

Although identified by a number of labels, management scientists today are usefully at work on a wide variety of business problems, ranging from inventory control to the long-term, unstructured strategic issues that senior executives traditionally handle. And, given the increasing complexity and rate of change in business, their place seems relatively secure: At the very least, their special value lies in the ability of MS to cut through complexity and to evaluate change in ways that reduce these inevitable problems to manageable proportions.

Yet, the actual domain and identity of management science are marked by uncertainties.

---

[1] Throughout this report the terms "management science" and "operations research" are used interchangeably, as they are in most contexts. For all practical purposes, whatever differences in meaning they may have had have long since dissolved. As a convenience, the abbreviations MS or OR or MS/OR, are frequently employed in place of the full names—and, similarly, without any particular significance.

For example, what areas of business decision making offer the most potential for the application of MS? What constitutes a comfortable, effective context for MS practitioners in an organization? What education and experience do – or should – these specialists have? Even though they and their work are well regarded by top management – as this report shows – many MS practitioners are unsure about management's acceptance of their work, the future of their field of expertise, and, therefore, of their careers. Ignorance exists among many members of the MS fraternity concerning the work of counterparts in other firms – ignorance about the kinds of projects being worked on, about the contributions being made to the well-being of their companies, and so on.

This report – essentially a survey of how MS is used and how it is faring in business today – is intended to clarify these uncertainties, so that MS can play an even more effective role. Informed users, such as general and functional managers or staff specialists like corporate planners, can also get clues on how to draw on MS techniques in fulfilling their own responsibilities.

The "Scientific Approach" of Management Science

At its simplest, management science/operations research is often defined as a "scientific approach" to problem solving for executive management. One difficulty of this definition seems to stem from management's popular conception of the "scientific approach." The term, of course, only refers to a process: (1) the careful observing of phenomena of interest; (2) the drawing of inferences about the nature of these phenomena from the observations; (3) the building of a theory describing or explaining the behavior of the phenomena; and (4) the making of additional independent observations of the situation in order to evaluate how well the theory does, in fact, predict or fit the continued behavior.

One can begin this cycle at any point. The essence of the scientific method lies in carrying out these repeated steps. Some business executives' notion that to do so implies converting the business or community into a laboratory is responsible for much of the confusion about MS/OR.

Business executives' reactions to the scientific method appear to run between two extremes. On one hand, many claim that they expect their managers to operate scientifically: "It's just common sense to expect responsible managers to observe operations under their control; to devise ideas of how they should operate and why; to make adjustments to bring their ideas and the operation into agreement; and then to observe how well their ideas fit the facts."

At the other extreme are attitudes like these: "Our managers are action takers; we can't afford to have them sitting around making scientific observations and building fancy theories."

Of course, both arguments are true as far as they go. Nearly all managers operate rationally with business problems and, yet, very few are rigorously systematic in the recording of observations, statements of operating theories, or the testing, refining, rejecting, and reinforcing of their business theories.

John G. Kemeny, now president of Dartmouth College, underlines the recursive process of the scientific method: "It starts with facts, ends in facts, and the facts ending one cycle are the beginning of the next cycle. A scientist holds his theories tentatively, always prepared to abandon them if the facts do not bear out the predictions. If a series of observations designed to verify certain predictions force us to abandon our theory then we look for a new or improved theory."[2]

The two extremes of business executives' reaction to the scientific method suggest two principal bases for the management scientists' efforts. First, MS practitioners possess a specialized scientific competence to carry out this rational approach – if not in the precise man-

[2] John G. Kemeny, *A Philosopher Looks at Science.* New York: Van Nostrand Reinhold, 1959, pp. 85-86.

ner of the laboratory scientist, then at least in methods appropriate to the more dynamic real-life environment of business. Second, as analyzers rather than performers, management scientists are in a position to concentrate on more systematic observations, hypothesis building (now more frequently called "model building"), testing and recycling in constructing their recommendations for the managements they serve.

The Domain of Management Science

After defining operating systems as those that involve men and machines operating in a natural environment (where the term "machine" may take on a meaning ranging from mechanical devices to complicated social mechanisms operating according to accepted rules), Professor Hugh Miser states: "In sum, operations research is a science because it employs the method of science to create its knowledge, and it is distinguished from other sciences by undertaking to account for the phenomena of operating systems, a context of nature largely neglected by other sciences."[3]

While this is a sufficiently precise statement of the status of MS/OR as a *science,* many businessmen feel that it falls short of defining the "context of business" into which MS/OR naturally fits. They perceive few business operating systems that are not already included in some well-established domain of managerial functions. Many of them – manufacturing operations, for example – already have well-settled subunits specifically assigned to the tasks of analyzing and improving, refining and, in general, rationalizing their operating systems. In manufacturing, such units are generally known as industrial engineering units. The concept of applying the scientific method also underlies the rationale for many of the marketing research units in business.

While it may be true that many of business'

operating systems exist in an environment free of continuing efforts organized for their analysis and improvement, the traditions of "territorial defense" die hard. An external analytical function designed to "help" the operators of these systems improve their performance is not always a welcome aid. Certainly, the operators of these systems might be justified in their resentment of an implicit assumption that their systems suffer from a neglect of study.

A Wider Disenchantment

To some extent, management science has shared the tarnished image that scientific endeavor in general bears at this particular juncture in history. Many factors, including the public discernment of pollution and other environmental ills, are perceived to be a consequence of untrammeled "scientific progress." The painful realization that the scientific methods that got men to the moon are as yet incapable of solving more immediate social and economic problems on earth contributes to a general decline in respect for science.

In exploring this disenchantment and looking for alternatives to problem discovery and solution, the industrial psychologist, Harold J. Levitt, discerns a difficulty in the training of management analysts. In attempting to nurture analytic *thinking* by developing and teaching analytic *techniques,* teachers have succeeded all too often, he believes, in producing skilled but empty number pushers. "By analytic thinking," Levitt says, "I mean more than a set of specific techniques; I mean a predominant style of thinking that is difficult to characterize completely but includes a preference for the language of numbers, a propensity to divide problems into components, to search for operational decision rules, and to search also for convergence – that is, for an answer."[4] Levitt points out that a professional need not be pigeonholed as either an "analytic thinker" or an "intuitive thinker." Obviously,

[3] Hugh J. Miser in *Handbook of Operations Research,* J. J. Moder and S. E. Elmaghraby, editors. New York: Van Nostrand Reinhold, (forthcoming).

[4] Harold J. Levitt, "Beyond the Analytical Manager," *California Management Review,* Spring No. 3, 1975, p. 6.

individuals may function in one way or another and still be perfectly capable of bridging both styles of thought. The management scientists surveyed were quite frank in discussing the clash between the two styles in their practice, however. They often balanced the positive attributes that they felt were associated with their analytical skills with the difficulties of communication. This will be discussed later in the study with more detail.

The Design of the Survey

The information upon which this report is based was gleaned from two major sources: (1) a two-phase research survey that was designed to obtain quantifiable estimates of MS practices across a broad business spectrum; and (2) a series of personal interviews. These ranged from an intensive examination of MS/OR units in their company settings to informal discussions of contemporary methods and approaches.

The first phase of the research effort was designed to identify and locate MS/OR units scattered over many industries: a screening questionnaire was addressed to senior personnel executives and sent to a sample of more than 1,250 firms. Of these, 492 responded.

For the purposes of the study, the following descriptions of (1) "management science," and (2) management science units were provided to the respondents:

(1) " 'Management science' refers to the systematic study of managerial systems, relying heavily on quantitative and mathematical analytical techniques."

(2) "A management science component is *any* staff unit established primarily to apply the tools and techniques of quantitative or mathematical analysis to the study and improvement of managerial systems."

The second phase involved a series of three questionnaires – each designed to collect data on general questions about MS/OR practice from the managers of a sample of the units identified in the screening phase. A total of

---

Definitions of Principal Company Characteristics Used in This Study

Company Size
- Large Companies – Companies having 50,000 or more employees
- Medium Companies – Companies having 10,000 to 49,999 employees
- Small Companies – Companies having fewer than 10,000 employees

Type of Business
- Nonmanufacturing – Agribusiness, mining-extraction, construction; SIC codes 01 through 17.
- Manufacturing– Manufacturers, SIC codes 20 through 39.

Industrial – Combined SIC codes 01 — 39

- Transportation/ Utilities – SIC codes 40 through 49.
- Trade/Services – Wholesale, retail trade (SIC codes 50 through 59), and hotels, amusements, recreation, etc. (SIC codes 70 through 79).
- Financial – Financial institutions, SIC codes 60 through 67.

Services – Combined SIC codes 40 — 79

---

296 managers responded to one or more of these instruments in the data collection phase ending in early 1976.

Firms to which the studied MS/OR units belonged were classified, for analysis purposes, as to size (number of employees), type of business (two-digit Standard Industrial Classification code), and geographic location (three-digit zip code). (See box on page 4.) In addition, other characteristics of the MS/OR units studied or their firms were derived from the response data for comparative analysis (age of unit, size of unit in terms of MS/OR professionals, organizational context, and so forth).

Chapter 2
Age and Origins of Management Science Units

THE OLDEST management science unit reported in the survey was about as old as a business management science group could be – 32 years – given that operations research/management science was unheard of until 1945, the year this unit was established. Mathematicians and actuaries who served with Dr. Phillip A. Morse in the U.S. Navy's operations research activity during World War II returned to a major insurance company and established a unit. The largest group of management science units studied were established before 1965. A minority (14 percent) of these units are made up of pioneering units established before 1955, close to the "watershed" years before which MS/OR activities were a rarity in business.[1]

A cumulative trace of the age distribution of MS units (see Chart 1) reveals that, after a scattered collection of companies began starting units (mostly in the nonmanufacturing

Chart 1: Cumulative Management Science Unit Distribution by Year of Establishment

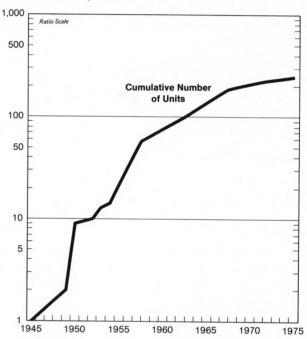

[1] The growth of professional societies in the field is another example of the marked shift in MS/OR activity around 1955. Prior to that year, only the Operations Research Society of America (1952), The Institute of Management Sciences (an international society, founded in the United States in 1953 and still predominantly North American in membership), and the British Operational Research Society (a 1953 successor to the Operational Research Club formed in 1948) had been established. Eight more national OR societies were formed from 1955 to 1960; since then, 20 or so other national groups have been formed. All of these, as well as some governmental and special interest groups, adhere to the International Federation of Operational Research Societies formed in 1959.

segment of the industrial sector, a segment which includes the oil companies) a general, rapid acceleration in unit establishment took place in the years spanning 1955 to 1964. Since then, growth in the number of firms establishing management science functions has continued more slowly, but at an even pace (see Table 1).

These data, of course, reflect the age distri-

Table 1: Age Distribution of Management Science/Operations Research Units by Size and Type of Business

| | Age of MS/OR Units Studied | | | |
	Young Established Since 1970	Medium Established 1965-1969	Old Established Before 1965	Total
Size of Company				
Large – over 50,000 employees	11%	23%	66%	100%
Medium – 10,000-49,999 employees	18	39	43	100
Small – under 10,000 employees	46	32	22	100
Type of Business				
Nonmanufacturing	14	14	72	100
Manufacturing	20	38	42	100
Industrial Average	19	34	47	100
Transportation/Utility	38	23	38	100
Trade/Service	50	31	19	100
Financial	34	44	22	100
Service Average	39	34	27	100
Overall Average	25	34	41	100

bution of units cooperating in this study; they do not, therefore, reflect the larger number of units established over this full period, some of which have been discontinued or dispersed.

Origins of Management Science Units

The executive most commonly identified as the principal initiator of management science/operations research activities in the firm is the chief executive officer, but this occurs in just 23 percent of the responding companies. A financial officer is almost as likely to have sparked the firm into taking this action (22 percent of the time).

A *group* of executives, however, all involved with technical support functions, receives 30 percent of the mentions as MS/OR initiators. These executives are in planning functions, the research and development organization, or the information systems and data processing function. This group also includes those units initiated by the current head of the MS/OR group – frequently an individual with MS/OR training or experience – who had succeeded in having his firm act upon his interest by establishing an MS/OR activity.

Another group, including marketing and manufacturing executives, accounts for 14 percent of the individuals credited with having initiated interest in the founding of an MS/OR group. Outside consultants are identified as the initiating source in less than 6 percent of the companies studied; the remaining firms admit they no longer remember how MS got started.

Reasons for Forming MS/OR Units

When asked what sparked the initial interest in the formation of an MS/OR group in their company, participants report that the most frequent motivation was a confrontation with a serious, pervasive or unusual problem that the initiating executive believed MS/OR could help solve. Other reasons given by MS unit managers are listed in descending order of frequency:

(1) A growing awareness of the problem-solving capabilities of MS/OR;

(2) A more generalized (i.e., not related to a specific problem) sense of need for improved problem-solving procedures;

(3) The recognition of an available internal nucleus around which to build an MS/OR function; and

(4) The recommendation of an outside management consultant.

A modest number of companies do not recall the specific motivations for starting an MS/OR unit. An even smaller group states that the beginning of MS/OR was simply related to keeping up with the Joneses: Management had heard that competitors or customers had such groups and felt that it should, too.

Specific Problems

According to the survey, the specific problems that triggered the establishment of an MS/OR activity fall into four major areas. In descending frequency of mention they are:

(1) Problems in the production-manufacturing and logistics management area;

(2) Planning and control problems;

(3) Critical cost or profit squeeze; and

(4) Difficulties experienced with the management and exploitation of information systems and data processing functions.

In the first area, problems of load forecasting, production planning, inventory management, and the perplexities of sorting out the economic implications of highly complex production-distribution systems are the specifics most often cited.

The need to establish better methods of evaluating strategies and tactics – from major investment alternatives to R and D project selection – is among the planning problems inspiring the creation of an MS activity. Equally as common is a more general need to improve the company's planning procedure, and the realization that a management science effort would aid such improvement.

Other planning and control-related problems leading to an MS activity include: "The desire of our management to expand and diversify." "The interest of our Controller in 'methods

improvement' and the need to find ways to handle the assimilation of more than 100 acquisitions in a little over ten years."

As for cost and profit influences, such citations as "reduced earnings," "the CEO needed to increase profits," and "it was seen as a means of cutting costs in operations," can be read either as specific problem motivations or as symptoms of a need for MS applications to improve planning and control systems.

The advent of computer-based information or data processing systems has led to the introduction of management science in firms. The associated demands for systems development and the design of procedures for providing management information – particularly that with a weightier or more insightful analytical content – have also contributed to the greater use of MS. A comment by a pharmaceutical company executive is typical: "The company faced two major information problems requiring MS/OR work: One was raising the competence of our computerized information systems to meet the increased demands due to rapid company growth; the other centered around a concern to develop techniques for production-control information systems."

More Generalized Needs

Many executives report that a management science activity was initiated in response to a generally felt need to upgrade the company's decision making. At one extreme, the motivation is stated that simply: "MS was started because we felt the need for a more structured decision-making process." At the other extreme, a company indicates that it felt the need "to develop a professional management team."

Other general needs mentioned by the surveyed companies include the growing complexity of business, the emergence of novel problems, rapid expansion, and, less specifically, a feeling of malaise from a sense of things slipping out of top management's control – thereby inducing an awareness of the necessity for new managerial procedures.

An Existing Nucleus

Another reason for the initiation of an MS activity is that "it just grew." Individuals, mostly within technical support functions, picked up MS tools and started applying them successfully to problems in the course of their work. As their – or their group's – reputation and usefulness grew, the ad hoc activity was formalized and a management science unit was established.

At the time of the survey, many of these groups still remained as subunits within the original technical functions in which they started. The evolution of such groups is typified by the report of one unit that grew from a nucleus within the data processing function. They report that the nucleus built "slowly in response to searches for special techniques to aid specific users who contacted data processing for computer assistance on their problems."

Chapter 3
Pros and Cons: Management Scientists Consider Their Strengths and Weaknesses

IN THE SURVEY, management science managers were not unwilling to be candid about both the positive and negative factors in the practice of their profession. Their remarks reflect the conflicts inherent in MS/OR's transition from what was seen originally as a rather glamorous panacea to what is now an acknowledged, yet still novel, problem-solving resource.

The Comments

Their comments have been grouped into a dozen or so positive and negative attributes of MS practice in general. For nearly every positive characteristic cited there is a criticism, but the executive who is expanding his or her knowledge of MS should find the professionals' own pros and cons to be valuable insights.

Comprehensive Evaluation versus Narrowness

The most frequently cited strength of MS practice is labeled its "comprehensive evaluation." This positive attribute stands directly opposed to "narrowness," the most frequently mentioned MS weakness. In examining the comments grouped under these opposites, one discerns underlying each attribute two subcategories or extremes of meaning. By "comprehensive evaluation," managers are

not only referring to the ability of MS to afford management the benefit of business situation models rich in detail – models taking varied factors into account, and representing situations from the "whole problem" perspective instead of parochial viewpoints. They are also referring to the other end of the process: Their ability to generate and analyze many more alternative solutions, and even to reveal unsuspected anomalies in situations that management might otherwise overlook.

"Narrowness" includes those comments about practitioners who feel obliged to warp all the problems they confront into a limited repertoire of MS techniques. The mention of "narrowness" also contains a realization that even the full range of current MS tools falls short of encompassing the entire scope of managerial problems.

Discipline and Control of Complexity versus Overkill

Two positive attributes MS managers mention almost as frequently as comprehensive evaluation are (1) the profession's ability to induce or impose *disciplined, rigorous thinking* about managerial problems; and (2) the profession's *taming of complexity*. With the same frequency, MS managers assert that a principal weakness is a tendency to use fancy means to solve problems – to *overkill* a problem by being too theoretical or academic.

Imposing a disciplined way of thinking "forces people to think completely and logically through a problem," says an MS unit head in a division of an agricultural equipment and supplies producer. He concludes that a better framework for improved decision making is thereby provided. Management science managers agree that this attribute tends to occur in two main ways. In one, MS practitioners themselves apply a characteristically scientific approach to problem solving as they impose order on vaguely structured situations. In another, many of the MS managers find that their own probing, logical approach to problem dissection and analysis rubs off on their management clients, thereby inducing more disciplined management discussions of problems. In any case, the very awareness of such disciplined thinking enhances management's understanding of the process.

Management science/operations research's ability to handle complexity was ascribed to the management scientist's special competence in working through extremely tangled situations, separating the critical from the irrelevant. This competence, called by a number of commentators management science's chief *raison d'être,* lies in the profession's capacity for the analysis and improvement of management systems embedded in complex environments.

The line between the virtue of the disciplined handling of complexity and the vice of using fancy solutions is a fine one. Sometimes, many managers agree, the pursuit of rigor degenerates into sophism. MS managers echo, in their own terms, the businessman's common concern about building products beyond the customer's need. Their criticisms run from overcomplication of a problem to overconcern with theoretical, ivory-tower trappings rather than with practical solutions to business problems. An oil company MS manager says: "There is a tendency to overly complicate the approach to a problem, resulting in reports on many elegant solutions that are promptly filed on management bookshelves and never used on problems by operating personnel."

Usefulness versus Impracticality

A number of MS managers mention the *usefulness* of their practice to management. In almost the same breath (certainly with virtually the same frequency) they decry the *impracticality* of some of their peers. In describing the usefulness of their efforts to business management, the MS managers use words like "speed," "accuracy," and "profitability" to describe the highly pragmatic values the practice of management science can bring to their firms. Often, they refer to the "quick and dirty" procedures that enable them to provide timely, effective and even inexpensive solutions to pressing problems.

On the other hand, managers also point out that many MS procedures can take too long, can cost too much, or can involve solution methods that lose sight of the results required by the eventual users. Some of them mention an excessive length of time for data collection, programming, problem formulation, and implementation, and indicate that they find management losing patience with prolonged MS projects. While MS practitioners report varying "attention spans" for their managements, it was rare to find any believing that these "attention spans" would extend much beyond a year; most successful practitioners try to avoid projects that take more than a few months without at least useful intermediate results.

A few MS managers mention a communications problem, ascribing an MS failure to appreciate business perspectives to a culture gap: MS professionals and their user-clients operate in different worlds and perceive each other in warped perspectives at times. The MS types see themselves as cool, rational "scientists," and their clients as "seat-of-the-pants gun-slingers." Their clients, on the other hand, view the MS specialists as impractical "eggheads" and themselves as hard-working businessmen with their feet on the ground.

One MS manager in a farm implement business agrees with others in laying this weakness to tendencies among MS practitioners to be "too academic, detached from reality; excessively preoccupied with theoretical considerations; guilty of using ill-defined terminology; accepting unjustified and undocumented assumptions; and tainted with incestuous clannishness." However, a number of MS managers believe that this disregard of business viewpoints is a common problem of professionals in industry, whose primary allegiance may be to their profession rather than to the enterprises they serve.

Some MS managers also admit that there are practitioners who are either too inexperienced or incompetent – or both – to function effectively. Some distinguished between what

---

Top Management Interest

The most important source of management science units' concern for top management interest is fairly obvious: Their budgets, in most cases, are directly related to top management's perception of the management science unit. (As defined in the survey, "top management" includes the president or the chief executive officer, the senior or executive vice presidents, group or division top executives, heads of major corporate components, and so forth.)

Somewhat less obviously, the political consequences of any expression of interest weaker than positive endorsement can lead to loss of access to problems and data, to a lack of cooperation from managers, and the with-

Chart 2: Reported Interest in Management Science among Top Management

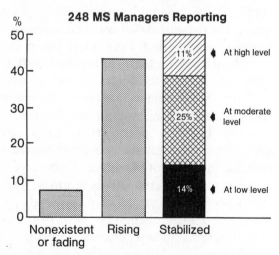

248 MS Managers Reporting

Chart 3: Reported Top Management Support for MS/OR

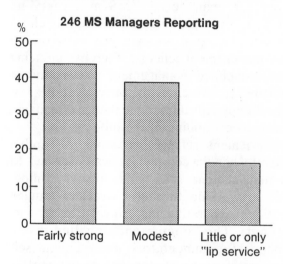

246 MS Managers Reporting

drawal of supporting resources, among other consequences.

Most managers find top management's interest in MS activities still rising or stabilized at moderate to high levels.

As Chart 2 shows, if the poorest levels of top management interest (the "nonexistent or fading" and the "stabilized at a low level") are combined, only about one-fifth of the MS managers perceive their top management as exhibiting weak interest in management science activities.

More importantly, most management science unit heads (83 percent) view their top management as giving them moderate to strong support, as Chart 3 indicates.

they call "people" skills – the ability to interact effectively with others, and technical skills – the ability to exploit effectively the tools of MS/OR. Closely related to the charge of a lack of professional acuity or experience was the celebrated "communications gap," part of the culture conflict mentioned earlier. MS managers deplore the *inarticulateness* of certain practitioners who find it difficult to explain their analyses or describe their solutions in the everyday language of business.

Other Criticisms of Management Science

Smaller numbers of managers mentioned these additional criticisms, which they feel a professional management scientist should make every effort to avoid.

• *Boat-rocking*. There is a tendency of MS practitioners to run afoul of organizational strictures, political structures, and businessmen's sensibilities. Some suggest that MS participation in a problem-solving project is often "requested" by top management, rather than by the real user-client; consequently, the MS staff occasionally finds itself perceived, at best, as top management's errand boys or, at worst, as corporate spies.

• *Overselling*. Some practitioners are said to be guilty of habitual overselling, over-promising, or raising expectations beyond the capability of the art or science of MS/OR (or any other!) to deliver.

• *Evaluation*. The frequent difficulty of assigning dollar values to MS benefits or the absence, in many cases, of easily identified payoffs, often provokes distress.

Executive Naivete

A detraction from the potential of MS practice as an aid to management, and one that was most frustrating to MS managers since it seemed to lie outside their influence, has been labeled *executive naivete*. This negative attribute was virtually the only one where MS managers placed most of the blame on the business managers they advise. Clearly the complement of MS practitioners' inarticulate-

ness, executive naivete refers to the apparent inability of many executives to accept mathematical methods, despite the clarity of language in which they are described. Particularly stifling to the MS practitioners is the suspicion of *mathematics* expressed by many general and middle management executives.

Undoubtedly, this weakness sometimes stemmed from management's lack of patience and understanding of MS procedures. It may even have masked procrastination when management did not feel like investing the time and effort required to bring MS professionals sufficiently into the situation to be solved. A possibly more alarming expression of this attribute is mentioned by a few MS professionals who report special concern with executives who accepted MS solutions blindly or on faith, not wanting to be bothered with the how-and-why of the solution process.

Most MS professionals take responsibility for bridging the communications barrier, wish as they might that management would try harder to meet them part way.

Another source of frustration to management scientists – one for which they did not always feel themselves to be at fault – is the difficulty of acquiring the data needed for their analyses and problem solving. Sometimes, they admit, elaborate models were conceived for which no appropriate data existed; more often, they implied, management looks with less than sympathy on new data collection efforts necessary to fully exploit the problem-solving potential of MS approaches. In a few other cases, MS managers hinted, practitioners are insufficiently familiar with company data sources.

Other Positive Attributes of Management Science

Ranking fourth in the managers' expressions of positive attributes of MS/OR practice is "quantification." This category covers not only the techniques that management scientists use to ascribe numerical values to difficult-to-measure, subjective, judgmental or conceptual values; it also covers the manage-

Constructive Reactions

There is no doubt that active MS practitioners are aware of the major weaknesses that erode their own and their clientele's confidence in their ability to be a significant aid to business decision making. What is less often mentioned are some of the constructive steps the MS professionals themselves are taking to overcome flaws and to remove the bases for the critics' complaints.

Rolled-up Sleeves

Disturbed by the lack of professional communication of demonstrably useful applications of MS/OR, members of the College on the Practice of Management Science (CPMS), a subdivision of The Institute of Management Sciences (TIMS), inaugurated an annual prize competition in 1971 for the best descriptions of the methods and results of successful MS/OR applications. Among other background data, submissions are required to include information permitting some independent verification of the actual results and benefits.

Initially setting a first-prize level of $200, the inaugurators, impressed with the difficulties and inhibitions that block submission of real life business applications papers, waited with trepidation. Eight papers were submitted. The following year, the first prize was raised to $500: about 20 papers were submitted. In the 1975 competition, the first prize was raised to $2,500, and nearly 100 papers were submitted. Winning papers are published in *Interfaces,* the informal quarterly journal of TIMS, published in cooperation with the Operations Research Society of America (ORSA).[1]

A parallel effort by the Business Applications Section (BAS) of ORSA seeks to recognize BAS members for exemplary applications descriptions, though without the prize money "carrot." Instead, the BAS council intends to seek wider distribution of these applications articles in leading business periodicals by providing editorial assistance to the contributors. They also plan to publish the articles in books of "executive readings in profitable business uses of operations research" and to assist the contributors in completing more comprehensive papers for publication in *Interfaces.*

Quick and Dirties

Along another track, there is the publication of "quick and dirty" solutions to common problems (often in manufacturing or production operations, distribution or logistics, marketing, and so forth). These are essentially short-cut solutions, often quick approximations rather than full-scale "optimizations," presumably accompanied by clear warnings about the hazards of ignoring the inherent limitations.

A sprightly collection of these solution methods is entitled *Operations Research for Immediate Application: A Quick and Dirty Manual.*[2] The senior author points out in the preface that this is, quite frankly, "a cookbook." He goes on to warn: "This means that using the recipes herein may cause acute corporate . . . indigestion if some careful thought is not given to the actual circumstances of the problem."

[1] For further information, write The Institute of Management Sciences, 146 Westminster Street, Providence, Rhode Island 02903; or, Operations Research Society of America, 428 East Preston Street, Baltimore, Maryland 21202.
[2] Robert E. D. Woolsey and Huntington S. Swanson, *Operations Research for Immediate Application: A Quick and Dirty Manual.* New York: Harper & Row, 1975.

ment scientists' ability to handle large amounts of quantitative data. A positive attribute complementary to quantification is labeled "MS tools," – that is, the power and value of the mathematical procedures used in MS practice. Some managers mention specific techniques that were proven especially useful in their practice.

Another positive attribute of MS practice, according to MS managers, is the *objectivity* they bring to their work. In one respect, this term refers to the MS unit's ability to cross internal lines, unaffected by "local" concerns. Most respondents, however, made it clear that they mean the individual practitioner's dedication to unbiased, nonintuitive observations of a situation. Sometimes, this attribute is described as the "freedom from company myths" – that is, the MS practitioner's unwillingness to accept passively "that's-the-way-it's-always-done-here" dicta, and insistence on testing company tradition for reasonableness, if not for truth.

Other favorable attributes mentioned by smaller numbers of MS managers included:

• *Talent*, the most self-adulatory attribute proposed by the managers, refers to the competence of MS practitioners, including their abilities to "recognize what is practical"; "handle analyses professionally, and also know what the business is all about"; "exhibit outstanding leadership qualities"; and "conceptualize and model business problems."

• *Involvement*, an attribute that describes the mutual involvement of the MS practitioner and the client in projects.

• *Teamwork*, meaning less the traditional multidisciplined approach to problem solving than it does the habitual business practice of establishing intracompany project teams with specialists selected from within the MS unit, the user-client organization, the finance-accounting staff, and so forth.

The Long View of Strengths and Weaknesses

With the clarity of hindsight, it is not surprising what possibilities for mutual disappointment have opened up for both the MS professional and his client. What is remarkable is that both have survived the initial shock. Some of the movement toward profitable accommodation is simply the reduction of a generational gap that inhibited easy and effective interchange between the MS practitioners and their management counterparts. Students who were in elementary school when Sputnik (1957) sparked

a revolution in mathematical education, are now entering the ranks of management, and are far less easily fazed by talk of matrices, probability theory, and LaGrangian multipliers. Management scientists, too, have learned to discuss double-entry bookkeeping and other bits of managerial semantics, as well as to comprehend that the "bottom line" is not just a kind of directed vector.

Furthermore, the ties between management science practitioners and business managers seem to have been strengthened by their experiences since 1973. In particular, tight money, material shortages, energy crises, rampaging inflation, and environmental impact concerns have brought the MS practitioners and their user-clients together to devise new solutions for handling these problems. For example, inventory control theories, long since developed far beyond the needs of an earlier time, suddenly came into prominence as both the costs of carrying and the values of inventories escalated precipitously after 1973.[1] Strategies for husbanding, acquiring and hedging raw material positions in radically shifting markets, as well as investment considerations under conditions of scarce capital availability and volatile demand, all have thrust the management scientists and their management counterparts into each others' arms during the past few years.

There is much evidence of the positive effects of MS efforts (as is apparent in the survey's list of projects that management scientists say contributed most to the firm's benefit and MS successes). A new maturity exists between general management and the management scientists as they work together to restructure and solve operational problems under unprecedented conditions.

[1] An oil company MS manager mentioned that, for many years, the factor of "working capital" in refinery operations – where it consisted largely of crude oil stocks – had virtually been ignored in routine refinery schedule optimizing procedures. After being allowed to rise and fall, willy-nilly, the suddenly inflated price of crude oil raised these stock values significantly. They became a prime minimization target as the refinery operators sought to hold the lowest possible crude stocks (i.e., working capital) consistent with their basic refining requirements.

Chapter 4
What Are the Projects That Management Science Is Doing?

MOST SERVICE UNITS or, for that matter, functional business groups seem to have an established basis by which they distinguish their domain – that unique *raison d'être* which their specialty contributes to the larger enterprise. In broad but recognizable terms, the domain of the personnel organization is the employees of a business; the intercourse of the company with its markets is the domain of the marketing function; and so on. Even these relatively well-defined domains often overlap, raising questions of territorial rights. But these territorial disputes seem relatively mild when compared with the drawing of boundaries between management science and other business functions.

What is the business territory of the management scientist in the corporate environment? What are the managerial problems that define the work space of management science? It has been suggested that the business problems which management scientists handle are the best guidelines for defining their domain. Several authors have offered clear boundaries to describe and characterize MS/OR in business, while others have added their opinions on where the most hospitable terrain might be found for MS practice.

Dimensions for a Map of Projects

One dimension suggested for a map of MS projects is the degree of structure associated with the problems encountered: Are the problems found in a highly structured state, with much knowledge and data available – perhaps, even with routines already established for rule-of-thumb solutions?[1] Or is the problem quite unstructured – a novel or unique situation with few hard details. This kind of problem may be fraught with unusual – even unpredictable – consequences. Most business problems can be arrayed, at least roughly, along such a structured-unstructured spectrum.

Another suggested dimension relates MS/OR problems to the ranking of managerial concerns or activities. Here, difficulties are arrayed from the daily "how-to-do-it" sort to the more global – the "what-should-we-be-getting-ready-to-do" variety involved with the broader aspects of business strategies. These two dimensions appear to have a natural relationship to each other. Usually the day-to-day operational problems are the more highly structured; the strategic problems tend to be far less so.

A third dimension of management science's domain – the major functions of a business – is marked by less than even the rough precision of the first two. Here it is suggested that the

[1] See Stanley J. PoKempner, *Information Systems for Sales and Marketing Management*. The Conference Board, Report No. 591, 1973, pp. 4-5.

more structured problems are most likely to be among the so-called operating functions of the business – in the production or manufacturing area, the distribution or logistics function, even in sales or marketing. General management might be expected to have problems that are more strategically oriented, less well-structured, less well-understood, and even more difficult to state – let alone solve. An example is illustrated in the paradox of the "Scientific Foreman and the Intuitive President" (see box), which suggests at least a crude agreement of this dimension with the first two degrees – structure and level of managerial activity.

Obviously, the correlation of this dimension with the other two is not along a straight line; strategic questions and problems arise on the factory floor on numerous occasions: when new production technology has to be confronted, for example, or when a new, unusual or revitalized class of customer appears. Similarly, more mundane, operational problems are not unknown even in the more rarified atmosphere of corporate headquarters.

The Projects of Management Science

In part, this survey was designed to explore from three major perspectives the projects on which management science units work. The first was *popularity over time:* "What projects has your unit worked on over the *past five years?*" "What projects is it working on in the last half of 1975?" "What projects do you expect it to be working on in the *future,* that is, in the next few years?"

In addition, the respondents volunteered project titles and identifying descriptions for two important qualitative attributes: (1) those MS projects in which the unit's performance had made the *greatest contribution* to the firm's well-being; and (2), those projects to which the senior MS staff members devoted the *closest attention* "now or over the past few years."

From these three major perspectives, the territory or domain within which MS activities took place can be described in greater detail.

The top 20 projects are ranked by: (1) popularity of projects being worked on; (2) greatest contribution; and (3), most attention. The rankings from survey results are enumerated in Table 2, page 18. Tables of all of the data on the popularity of projects – past, present and future – and the projects nominated as making the greatest contributions and receiving the most attention will be found in Appendix A, pages 52-55.

The Paradox of the Scientific Foreman and the Intuitive President

"There is a curious natural law in business that places a premium on managerial imagination – The Bigger the Problem the Fewer the Facts. This law manifests itself in the necessary paradox of the 'scientific foreman and intuitive president.' Many problems at the supervisor's level can be quantified, analyzed and optimized down to the last few percent – problems in production scheduling, make-or-buy, even allocating salesmen's time to customers. But most problems at the president's level involve such intangibles that any decision at all takes courage. For instance, the problems of whether or not to build a plant, or how to build the plant, are of completely different orders of magnitude.

"Thus, this simple law places increasing emphasis on the art of sensing essentials early, of drawing inferences from barely sufficient information. For example, a major decision, by the time it is supported by a solid factual basis, in all likelihood should have been made several years ago! Such an art places an increasing burden on the managerial imagination – not in imagining nonexistent facts, but in erecting, demolishing and re-erecting conceptual structures to organize and use the few facts available as intelligently as possible."

Harlan D. Mills, *Mathematics and the Managerial Imagination.* Princeton, N.J.: Mathematica, Inc., 1959, page 1.

Table 2: Top 20 Management Science Projects Ranked by Popularity, Greatest Contribution, and Most Attention

Project Application Areas	Major[1] Functional Area	(A) Actively Engaged in Now[2]	Projects Mentioned as: (B) Making the Greatest Contribution to the Firm (Ranks)	(C) Receiving the Most MS Group Attention (Ranks)
Corporate Planning Models	GM	1	2	2
Cash-Flow Analysis	FIN	2	17*	17.5*
Long-range Financial Forecasting	FIN	3	19.5*	19
Inventory Management	LOG	4	3.5*	4
Long-range Economic Forecasting	GM	5	9*	8*
Production Planning	MFR	6	1	1
Investment Analysis	FIN	7	14	13
Capital Budgeting	FIN	8	#	14.5*
Financial Information Systems	FIN	9	9*	8*
Generating Strategy Alternatives	GM	10	#	#
Facilities Planning	GM	11	3.5*	6
General Management Information Systems	GM	12	#	#
Budgeting and Control	FIN	13.5*	9*	10.5*
Production Scheduling	MFR	13.5*	15	14.5*
Marketing Research	S/M	15	5	3
Developing Plans	GM	16	#	#
Pricing Studies	S/M	17	9*	10.5*
Strategy Evaluation	GM	18	#	#
Marketing Strategy Analysis	S/M	19.5*	12.5*	17.5*
Marketing Information Systems	S/M	19.5*	#	#
Production Methods Research	MFR	#	6	5
Risk/Venture Analysis	FIN	#	9*	8*
Physical Distribution	LOG	#	12.5*	12
Portfolio Analysis	FIN	#	17*	#
Storage/Distribution Facilities Planning	LOG	#	17*	16
New Product Analysis	S/M	#	19.5*	20

* Indicates tie in rank in same column. Ranks shown for tied items are the *average of the ranks* that would have been assigned if the values of the tied items had differed slightly from each other.

\# Not ranked within top 20.

[1] Abbreviations: FIN = Finance; GM = General Management; LOG = Logistics (Distribution); MFR = Production (Manufacturing); S/M = Sales/Marketing.

[2] Last half of 1975.

The "Shopping List" of Project Areas

A "shopping list" of some 60-odd principal project or application areas (with ample space for "other" projects or applications to be reported) was provided to survey participants. In effect, the popularity of past, present and expected MS projects was to be ascertained by their selections. The project list was grouped into six management application areas – business functional categories in which preliminary research had shown MS units to be engaged: finance, general management, logistics (distribution), personnel, production (manufacturing), and sales and marketing. The importance of these major application areas to management science practice can be estimated from the net incidence of MS/OR units actively engaged in each principal area. Essentially, this analysis counted the units reporting active engagement in at least one project area within each of the major functional categories.

The general management area headed the application areas, with over 90 percent of the units reporting at least one project under way that guided top management decisions. Second in importance was finance, with about 86 percent of the units actively engaged in one or more projects. Over two-thirds of the MS units worked on projects in the sales and marketing area; about 60 percent worked in production; and about 55 percent worked in logistics. Only in personnel did less than a majority – but still over 40 percent of the MS units – report that they had active projects under way. A sprinkling of units reported projects applying management science to improved research and development decision making.

By and large, the rank order of popularity did not shift in any dramatic way over the past-present-future listings, although there were changes, at the lower order of the ratings. As expected, the absolute numbers of mentions were greater for past and future projects since these covered greater time spans than projects being worked on "now."

A "Mixed-Bag" Domain

The first half-dozen project areas ranked initially by their order of popularity (as of the last half of 1975) reveal the scatter of problem-solving efforts over the management science domain. These application areas range from the mainly strategic and relatively unstructured issues of corporate planning and long-range financial and economic forecasting, through cash-flow analysis, to the well-documented and more operationally oriented issues of inventory management and production planning. Some of these applications may vary in structure; for instance, cash-flow analysis may involve the vaguely structured considerations of far-term flows as well as the more nearly operational issues of near-term cash-flow problems.

Even more indicative of the mixed bag of MS/OR problem-solving efforts are the fairly radical shifts in ranks among the top ten "popularity" projects. This occurred when the qualitative aspects of "concentrated attention" and "corporate contribution" were taken into account. Only five of the ten most popular project areas rank within the top ten on all three measures (corporate planning models, inventory management, long-range economic forecasting, production planning, and financial information systems). Cash-flow analysis and long-range financial forecasting barely stayed within the top 20 of the projects when ranked by the two qualitative indicators. To underscore the pervasiveness of MS/OR activities, two of the project areas highest in popularity are in general management application, two are in the financial area, and one each is in the logistics and distribution as well as the production-manufacturing area. The two project titles in the financial area drop completely out of the top-ten ranks when measured by the qualitative dimensions.

Corporate Planning Models

Projects involving *corporate planning models,* applied in the general management area, lead the entire list in popularity, past, present and future. A clear majority (56 percent) of MS units were actively engaged in building or exercising mathematical models (most likely simulations) in support of corporate planning activities during late 1975. About 63 percent had been so engaged sometime during the preceding five years, and 73 percent expected to be doing so during the next few years. These results seem not to vary with the characteristics of the firms. Large or small, industrial or service businesses – all reported corporate planning models as a popular MS activity.

Overall, corporate-planning model activity rates very high among the project areas that receive high attention and contribute significant benefits to the company, ranking second in both of these important qualitative aspects. Among smaller firms, this project area was rated first, both in the amount of attention given and in the degree of contribution. In larger firms, where this activity perhaps had been pursued longer, corporate-planning model activity received somewhat less attention and was rated below several other projects in contribution value, although it was still among the top activities.

Cash-Flow Analysis

A gap of ten percentage points separates the top-ranked popular project area from the second – *analysis of cash flows* (46 percent). As an area of MS activity in the recent past, this financial application enjoyed the same popularity and was expected to continue high on the list of areas which would engage MS units in the future.

Long-Range Financial Forecasting

Only slightly lower in interest (44 percent) was MS activity in those projects involved with the development of *long-range financial forecasting* procedures. Active work in this field, designed to give firms a clearer glimpse into the important financial variables of the future, rose to become the third-ranked project, MS units reported, having ranked this project seventh in the recent past.

The popularity of long-range financial forecasting projects gained as the size of the firm declined, and was slightly lower among industrial businesses than service business companies.

Inventory Management Projects

Inventory management projects, the fourth-ranked among the projects MS units were aiding in late 1975, would certainly be regarded by most management scientists to be a relatively well-structured, operational problem. Inventory management projects were slightly less popular than in the preceding five years (ranked third), and they are expected to decline further, to sixth or seventh place in the future. Interest in this logistics application declined markedly as the size of company declined.

As might be expected, industrial firms and retail and wholesale trading businesses were much more likely to have had a high interest

in physical inventory problems. Inventory management projects were often mentioned by MS units to be contributing important benefits to their firms, and in this value measurement they tie for third place.

Long-Range Economic Forecasting

Projects in *long-range economic forecasting* are fifth in frequency for MS units during the last half of 1975. They had been rated much lower (tied for 13th) earlier. The relative importance of economic forecasts – a clearly strategic portion of the MS map – should stay at, or slightly above, this level, perhaps rising to fourth place in projects that MS units expect to be involved in during the next several years.

The hypothesis exists that the projection of economic variables is of most importance to those firms that are most influenced by them: companies that are of sufficient magnitude, in turn, to have an influence on the future course of these variables. Long-range economic forecasting was indeed more active in the MS units of larger firms than in those of smaller ones – the frequency declined with size across the board. Similarly, those firms whose planning horizons reach somewhat farther into the future – such as industrial firms and the transportation or utility sector – ranked this activity higher than did trade-service firms with their closer horizons.

Production Planning

MS projects in *production planning* appear to lie more in the operational-structured region of MS, although such projects could conceivably range to the strategic-unstructured end. This application area of projects undertaken for production or manufacturing management ranked sixth among projects occupying MS units. Industrial firms, of course, reported projects in this area much more frequently than did firms in the service sector, where the ''production function'' is less uniformly defined. Part of this difference may lie in the variety of businesses (transportation, utilities, banks, insurance companies, wholesale and retail trade firms, and so forth) included in the service classification. Perhaps of greatest importance is the fact that, among the MS unit heads surveyed, production planning was the number-one project area for both the amount of attention committed and for the contribution it made to their business' well-being.

Investment Analysis and Capital Budgeting

Two project areas closely related in substance and analytical approach – *investment analysis* and *capital budgeting* – rank seventh and eighth, respectively, with reference to popularity. These two were separately identified in the list presented to MS unit heads for their indication of past, present and expected future activity. Although these two project areas seem to be virtual duplicates, the evidence of the survey confirmed the propriety of listing both: Among financial service firms, investment analysis was the far more popular MS project area. Among manufacturing firms, for example, capital budgeting projects – properly a subset of the broader area of investment decisions – were just slightly more popular (44 percent, as compared with 38 percent). Investment analysis projects ranked 14th among projects credited with impressive contributions.

Information Systems Projects

Management science units are engaged in supporting the development of management information systems in all areas. To a large extent, this represents an acknowledgment of management science's capacity to enhance the value of data through the design of improved methods of analysis and inference. These provide sharpened insights and perceptions for decisions makers.

This is especially true in the project areas of *financial information systems* and *general management-information systems* ranked ninth and twelfth respectively, among projects in which MS units were actively engaged at the time of the survey. Expectations of future activity ranked about the same as the "present" ranks for the financial systems and somewhat lower for general MIS.

While MS units were engaged in projects to improve information systems in the logistics, production-manufacturing, and personnel areas, all of these efforts were ranked well below the financial, general and marketing management-information-systems areas. Only in the financial application area did information systems work rate highly, either as a source of beneficial contributions to the firm (tied for ninth) or as to resource commitment by MS units (tied for eighth).

Generating Strategy Alternatives

One of the less structured strategic tasks of general management in which MS/OR units participate is that of *generating strategy alternatives*. For example, a re-examination of a firm's major basic competencies and resources may give rise to questions about alternative strategies that would best exploit the company's strengths and mitigate – or even overcome – any weaknesses. Such questions require mathematical ingenuity or, at the least, a careful tracing of the strategic logic involved, and also considerable imagination. Vision is crucial to the generation of exhaustive alternatives – especially if the ultimate strategy decision will be made from among them.

Given the recent dramatic changes in business conditions, it is not surprising that this project area's popularity seems to be growing. The survey shows a growth – from below the top twenty in the past to tenth place in the present, as well as a tie for ninth place in the expectations of future project engagement. The generation of additional strategy alternatives is a project area in which MS units were called to help slightly more often in larger firms than in smaller; somewhat fewer service firms than industrial ones sought MS support in this area as well. Interestingly, management science units neither devoted a great deal of effort to generating strategy alternatives, nor did they believe that much in the way of contributions could be readily discerned.

MS Project Range in an Individual Company: Three Cases

In the aggregate, MS units exhibit a broad range of project management. Many of the projects in the areas of management most heavily reported by MS units – the general management and financial applications areas, for example – are of quite universal interest. On the other hand, many MS units frequently find their project range extended by the need to cover project areas that are of specific interest to the industries to which their firms belong. The three minicases described below typify how industry-specific needs can extend the range of MS unit engagement.

A Major Style Goods Manufacturer

While this firm's MS unit has worked in all areas of the firm, much of its effort is concentrated in the marketing or sales, general management, and finance areas. Some of its major projects have involved: (1) inventory and production analysis for closer control of the firm's widespread production and distribution facilities; (2) experimentation with computer-readable product labeling in order to create more efficient data generation and control for sales and distribution-information needs; and (3) a data-exchange program with buyers for a faster and more sensitive response to changing market conditions, as well as for improved customer services. In addition, the MS unit has aided the company in projects that ran the gamut from improved planning procedures to designing specific quality-control procedures.

During their work on inventory and production analysis, the unit developed a model based on product characteristics that they call "salability factors." These monitor current apparel inventories – which are especially vulnerable to volatile fashion trends – with an eye to potential mark-down risks. The success of this model now has the MS/OR group worried that managers may be delegating too much responsibility to the model and its monitoring function and not keeping their own eyes peeled for new salability factors that the model cannot "see."

A combination of the mark-down analysis model and an inventory/production/sales model that provides measurement criteria for the analysis of turnover rates has been implemented on a conversational-mode computer basis. Through the managers' computer terminals, this combination permits them to ask their own "what-if" questions. The managers can introduce product revisions and variations to the model, which then responds with pro forma profit and loss statements for the evaluation of the proposed changes.

The MS/OR manager of the firm indicates that much of the unit's success has been based on its own market-orientation: "We work hard at being responsive, recognizing our clients' needs, doing a professional – that is, a *good* – job, being innovative, taking a corporate view, in short, bringing many factors from many areas to bear on a problem, and adding our own technical expertise and ability to work with others in a mutually pleasant way." He noted that his unit avoided over-sophisticated models because of a conviction that the "softness" of data in the apparel industry would not support such efforts with the requisite accuracy or reliability.

A Major Airline

Like most other MS units studied, the airline's MS concentrated a considerable portion of its efforts on general management project areas, especially in planning. Unlike most other management science groups studied, however, the personnel area was the subject of the second largest number of MS projects. One of its major successes involves a manpower planning project designed to improve customer service levels while reducing work force requirements.

Marketing and finance are also areas of considerable MS effort, while the production management and logistics areas account for a relatively few – but often quite important – projects. For example, those projects regarding the management of some of the firm's most valuable assets – passenger-seat capacity and route schedules – were among the most important undertaken by operations research and development in terms of effort, contribution and recognition. A project to enable the airline to improve fuel utilization levels was also rated high on the unit's list of successful accomplishments. In recent years, the operations research and development unit graduated five of its members into management positions, including a company vice presidency.

A Chemical Company

The MS/OR group of six professionals in this firm concentrates, as do most MS/OR units, on relatively short-term projects whose average time runs under three months. These efforts, of course, include a large number of what the MS director described as "over-the-transom" jobs that might take only a few days or, at most, a few weeks to complete. By spreading the group's efforts over a wide panoply of management areas, the group has steadily rebuilt an originally negative image to the point where its acceptance is strong and constructive across most management levels.

Underlying the OR group's improved influence is a conscious acceptance that the firm's management is a sophisticated, technically competent group of individuals who, from time to time, may need more specialized guidance in improving their decision making.

Among the projects recognized as occupying the OR unit's attention most heavily and having resulted in significant contributions to the firm are these:

• A re-examination of inventory management policies and procedures. This review was done in the light of rapidly escalating demands for working capital to support the newly inflated costs of retail chemical products. High availability levels for these products are traditional marketing requisites.

• A study of interaffiliate pricing, done to determine the profit sensitivity of pricing policies to tax incidence factors compared with market demand factors.

• A project resulting in a large-scale simulation model used for evaluating the sales and profit contributions to be expected from one of the company's research laboratory's budget and forecasts.

• A study of the potential for sales synergism in the customer overlap among several divisions that are selling different products to what is essentially the same industrial trade.

• A successful application of a model for the location of warehouses and distribution facilities.

• The development of a simulation model that permitted salesmen, through the use of a conversation-mode terminal, to enter customer specifications for industrial chemical treatment systems. The salesmen could then manipulate the specifications to generate balanced configurations of their company's equipment that yielded the desired chemical levels while minimizing either the total equipment costs, the operating costs, or the present value of the investment.

The MS unit also performed more or less continuous work on improving the company's marketing support systems and its various forecasting procedures.

In this respect, generating strategy alternatives was one of several project areas – recognizable as activities undertaken deep in the strategic-unstructured zone of the MS domain – where apparent popularity, as judged by frequency of involvement, diverges sharply from qualitative rankings on the degree of attention or of contribution to the company. In this case, where mental acuity and individual creativity may count for more than formal project effort, substantial commitment to projects for strategy alternatives may seem inappropriate. Correspondingly, the gains to the firm from the development of a list of alternatives (as well as from other projects involving similarly unstructured, strategic issues – capital budgeting, for example) may be difficult to identify, let alone measure. Then, too, the reaping of the benefits may occur so distantly from the project's completion as to render a reasonable attribution of the benefits impractical.

Facilities Planning Projects

Improving the decision making necessary to detail the specifications of a new facility is much closer to the operational-structured axes than is the original "go-no go" question. *Facilities planning* projects rank 11th among MS applications areas, though they ranked higher in the past (fourth) and are expected to do so again in the future (tied for seventh). They also tied for third place in contributions to the firm and are sixth in attention given.

Most MS work in this area helps general management to improve decision procedures for the many questions of site selection, construction, acquisition, rehabilitation and so forth. Some of these questions, of course, involve longer range, even strategic, considerations as well. One example is when a level of technology has to be selected and "frozen" into the plans. Both the more general facilities planning (third place in contribution to the firm) and the logistics facilities areas (17th place in contribution) were slightly more popular among the larger and the industrial firms than among the smaller and service ones.

Facilities planning projects, either general or specific, exhibit the other side of the phenomenon noted above in the discussion of projects for generating strategy alternatives. That is, these projects at the operational-structured corner of the MS domain receive disproportionately *more* attention and generate *more* benefits than their popularity ratings would indicate. In contrast with the generation of strategic alternatives, for example, these more highly structured and near-operational decisions induce greater resource commit-

ment. At the same time, benefits to the firm are more amenable to measurement, more quickly realized, and more readily attributable to the planners in these projects than in the more strategically oriented ones.

Budgeting and Control

Helping to monitor the financial results of operations involves management science units in *budgeting and control* projects frequently enough to bring this area to a tie for 13th place in the popularity ranks. (A corollary area, *accounting systems,* ranked below the top 20.) Management science units in service businesses engaged more actively in both project areas than those in industrial firms.

The Remaining Project Categories

Beyond the first dozen project categories, the remaining areas divide equally into structured and unstructured zones of management science. In general, MS involvement in more strategic projects grows as the size of the firm increases. Neither the categories of *developing plans* (where MS units provide support for setting priorities or initiating studies for planning) or *strategy evaluation* receive enough mention, however, to put them in the top 20 for unit attention or contribution to the company. Marketing strategy analysis, basically an application area closely related to strategy evaluation, but more specifically focused in concern and time, did tie for 17th place in attention and benefit to the firm.

As might be expected, the operational areas of *production scheduling, pricing studies,* and *marketing research* rank higher than strategic categories in corporate contribution and attention given. With its potential for significant impact on business revenues, the field of pricing studies is tied for ninth place in contribution to the firm and tenth among those given closest attention. The incidence of marketing research projects increases as the company's size decreases, and manufacturing, utility and transportation firms account for slightly higher proportions of MS effort here than do other businesses. Management science attention to this application area put it in third place; and marketing research projects received enough citations for corporate contribution to rank it fifth in the survey.

Again, this area encompasses many well-structured, heavily operational issues – the very problems likely to be short-term and to have attributable and identifiable benefits. Many marketing research projects involve sales-forecasting improvements as well as other market monitoring systems with relatively straightforward project commitments that allow observation and measurement of results. At the other extreme, however, marketing research projects may also cover elaborate inferential means of evaluating the size and relative value of market segments, or measure indirectly the buying behavior of consumers or industrial customers. While potentially capable of providing valuable guidance, these marketing research projects do not lend themselves as easily to the estimation or crediting of benefits.

Beyond the Survey: Another Project Area

One other area, not listed in the original suggestions offered to MS units but written in by a number of MS managers, is that of consulting on analytical, statistical or mathematical techniques. Most often mentioned were projects involving statistical theory, especially experimental design and probability theory. The MS managers indicate that they serve as technical consultants to other groups needing special assistance while working on substantive issues surrounding particular problem areas. This kind of MS support is usually performed in projects under the general responsibility of groups either in research and development organizations or in projects for groups in marketing or personnel functions.

In the technique-oriented consulting efforts of the management scientists, the MS/OR content seems to fall beyond the dimensions of any recognizable business domain. Apart from the structured-unstructured, the operational-strategic, or even the functional zones, these largely methodological tasks make management scientists advisers to advisers, and at least one step further removed from "the action."

Areas Excluding Management Science

Besides the issue of defining the business areas in which MS units were actively using their skills, MS managers were asked about application areas in their own firms or in general business practice where they believed that it would be difficult for MS to make a significant contribution.

It is the opinion of over 86 percent of the MS managers that there is no specific area in which it proves difficult to establish MS's worth. About a fifth of this majority pointed out that many business problems exist where MS efforts might prove marginal but, at the same time, they deny that any specific area of business could not profit from MS practice. In these marginal cases, they explained, the problems were either so fleeting or small, or so gigantic or vacuous, that the effort required to mount an MS project would overwhelm any expected benefits. A few participants also mentioned the less-than-welcoming attitudes of certain individuals in their companies, without stating flatly that these individuals actually barred specific areas from MS practice.

The Management Role in the Organization

Part Two
The Management Scientist in the Organization

Chapter 5
The Education and Experience of Management Science Professionals

Not surprisingly, management science practitioners in the business units studied reflect a concentration of formal training (principal major fields of undergraduate or graduate education) in quantitatively oriented disciplines.[1]

The Formal Training of Management Scientists

The largest group of practitioners – 230 out of a total of 743 – reported degrees in one or more of the mathematical sciences, with or without another major field (see Table A-3 Appendix A). In fact, a majority of this group stated that they have degrees solely in the mathematical sciences.

The next largest set of practitioners (216) have at least one degree in business (finance, accounting, business administration), with just over half of this group concentrating only within this category. Half of these, in turn, have the popular Master of Business Administration (MBA) degree. And most MBA programs now include solid requirements in quantitative methodology. Those who also have a major or degree in another principal field besides business fall into a distribution pattern that is fairly even among the social sciences and humanities, engineering and science, mathematical and management science categories.

Of those professionals reporting a degree or major in the management sciences field, however, only about 40 percent concentrated solely within this category. Virtually equal numbers among the rest possess additional majors in business, engineering and science, or mathematical sciences; just a few also have majors in the social sciences or humanities. Nearly 60 percent of the MS professionals who have completed engineering and science majors have taken degrees only in these fields. Most of the remaining professionals with a major in this category also report degrees in the management sciences or in business curricula. The smallest group of practicing management scientists consists of those with a degree in the social sciences or humanities; among these, more than half took degrees in the field of economics, including the popular specialty of econometrics.

[1] The educational majors of professional MS/OR personnel are grouped into five general categories. Of these, Business Curricula, Engineering and (hard) Science, and Social Sciences and Humanities cover fairly obvious majors. The Management Science grouping includes both management science and operations research majors and industrial engineering. The latter field is most often described by MS managers as being more like the first two majors than other engineering disciplines. In addition to mathematics majors, Mathematical Sciences includes actuarial science, computer science and statistics.

Changes in Specialization Patterns

When management science practitioners are put into two major groupings – "juniors" and "seniors" – a marked shift in the patterns of formal preparation for the field is observable, at least to the extent that this arbitrary grouping reflects age differences.[2]

Among the senior practitioners, the greatest concentration of professional training is in the engineering and hard science majors (excluding industrial engineering). (See Table A-3, Appendix A.) Indeed, nearly a quarter (24 percent) of all the senior practitioners (excluding the unit managers) completed their formal education in majors *solely* within these specialties, all of which traditionally require a rich background in mathematics. An additional 12 percent included a science or engineering degree in their background *plus* another major.

In the numerically larger class of juniors, the engineering and science category is rated well below the fields of mathematical studies, business administration, and the management sciences. Indeed, the most dramatic difference between the two groups lies in the ranking of the mathematical sciences and the engineering and science areas: Mathematics ranks *first* among the juniors and *fourth* among the seniors; science and engineering, on the other hand, ranks *first* among the seniors and *fourth* among the juniors, when taking into account both the single and multiple majors groups. Relatively more junior than senior MS professionals mentioned a degree in the business curricula, reflecting the increasing popularity of the quantitatively oriented MBA degree.

Educational Background of MS Managers

Managers of management science units display another distribution of formal training.

Over half of the initial degrees that they reported (53 percent) are in the engineering and physical sciences curricula. (See Table A-3, Appendix A.) Indeed, as Chart 4 shows, two-fifths of *all* the degrees acquired by the managers reporting are in the engineering and physical science areas.

Other salient characteristics about the background of MS managers are these:

- Of those taking an undergraduate degree in engineering and science, the largest group has continued earning advanced degrees, mostly in the same category. They are followed by managers who earned advanced degrees in either the business curricula (mostly MBA's) or in management sciences.
- All of the managers initiating their formal education in the business curricula completed it in the same field.
- Over half of all business curricula degrees (55 percent) were preceded by initial degrees taken in other disciplines.

Chart 4: Summary of 135 MS Managers' Initial and Advanced Degrees

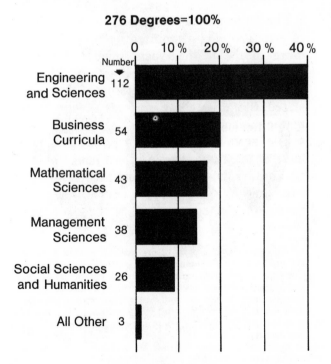

276 Degrees=100%

---

[2] For the purposes of description, management scientists other than MS managers are arbitrarily classified as "seniors" if they earned $25,000 or more annual base salary in 1975. When compared with the "least-experienced professional," "middle-level professional," and "top-level professional" classifications used in studying MS practitioner compensation, the junior and senior classes seem accurate, in addition to having generational relevance.

• In addition to at least one bachelor's degree, four out of five MS managers have masters; one out of five has a doctorate and another one out of seventeen has completed all requirements for the Ph.D. but the dissertation.

Experience of MS Managers

Half of the managers of MS units had been in the top spot for three years or less at the time of the survey, and only a quarter of them had been in this position six or more years, as of mid-1975, as Chart 5 shows.

Most attained their post by promotion within their present companies. As Chart 6 shows, half of them have been with their present companies more than eight years.

In their years with their present firms, prior to becoming head of the management science unit, most of the managers (63 percent) had had experience in at least one other area of the

Chart 5: Years as Management Science Managers

141 Managers Reporting =100%

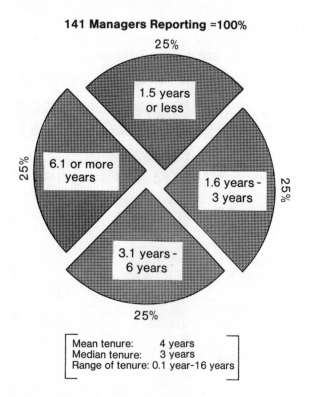

Mean tenure:	4 years
Median tenure:	3 years
Range of tenure:	0.1 year-16 years

Chart 6: Years with Present Company

141 Managers Reporting=100%

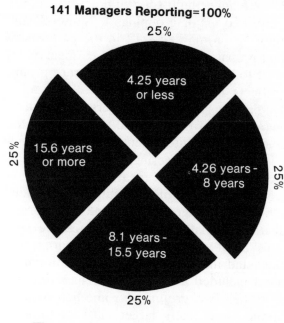

Mean tenure with present firm:	10.5 years
Median tenure with present firm:	8 years
Range of tenure:	1-39 years

business. Over half of these managers had worked in one of the complementary fields of management information systems or data processing, research and development, or planning.

Nearly four-fifths of the managers had had experience with one or more other employers before joining their present company. Of these, over a fourth had previously been in management science units; just over a third had worked in management information systems and data processing, R and D, or planning functions.

Most of the rest had worked principally in finance, marketing, manufacturing, or distribution. However, a sizable fraction (about one-third) of these managers who had worked for previous employers had been employed in institutions in the consulting field, in public agencies, and in academic or other nonprofit organizations.

Table 3: Total Annual Compensation of Management Science Professionals (to nearest thousand dollars)[1]

	Professional Categories			
	Least Experienced	Middle Level	Top Level	MS/OR Unit Managers
Average (mean) Annual Gross	$16,000	$23,000	$30,000	$38,000
First Quartile (Lowest 25 Percent)	14,000	19,000	25,000	28,000
Median (Point of 50/50 Division)	16,000	22,000	29,000	35,000
Third Quartile (Lowest 75 percent)	18,000	26,000	35,000	43,000
Range	10,000 to 27,000	11,000 to 37,000	13,000 to 53,000	18,000 to 113,000

To aid in the interpretation of these figures, the distribution of *highest* earned degrees in each of the categories is presented:

	Least Experienced		Middle Level		Top Level		Unit Head	
	Number	Percent	Number	Percent	Number	Percent	Number	Percent
Bachelor's Degrees	68	45%	90	31%	40	21%	28	20%
Master's Degrees	62	41	170	58	108	57	78	56
Doctoral Degrees	6	4	30	10	36	19	27	19
No degree reported	14	9	4	1	6	3	6	4
Totals	150	100%	294	100%	190	100%	139	100%

Note: Details may not add to 100 percent because of rounding.

[1]Includes salary plus bonuses, incentive pay, profit-sharing, and so forth, as appropriate.

Compensation of MS/OR Professionals

To focus on the sometimes complicated questions of compensation, managers of MS/OR units classified their professional personnel into three major groupings to assure at least broad comparability:

(1) Least-experienced professionals – those recently starting with little or no prior business experience, usually working under relatively close supervision.

(2) Middle-level professionals – those with significant time on the job with the company, or significant prior experience, usually working under relatively loose supervision.

(3) Top-level professionals and supervisors – those considered "lead" professionals or supervisors of MS/OR work, with significant experience and/or competence.

The managers also reported on their own compensation.

The total annual compensation figures in Table 3 are as of mid-1975 and include salary plus bonuses, incentive pay, profit sharing, and so forth, as appropriate.

Chapter 6
The Composition, Incidence, and Organizational Setting of Management Science Units

MANAGEMENT SCIENCE UNITS, measured by the number of full-time professional members reported in the survey, tended to be fairly small and composed of individuals with mathematically oriented backgrounds. Both the unit sizes and the professional qualifications seem at first to fall short of the classical prescription for a proper management science team: to provide a sufficient diversity of disciplined perspectives to heighten the chances of reaching useful solutions.[1] When other (non-MS) professionals are attached to the unit and a project task force is created – often composed of a mix of individuals from the MS unit, the user-client organization, and other experts – the major requirements of the classical model are probably fulfilled.

Size of Management Science/Operations Research Units

Including the unit head, the average MS/OR unit in the companies studied consisted of six management science professionals. Units ranged in size from one-man shops to those with 31 professionals. The most consistent correlate of size of the MS unit is, of course, the size of the company in which it is located, with the largest companies having the largest units, and the smaller companies, the smallest. (See Table A-4, Appendix A.)

Within the two major business sectors (industrial and service), the nonmanufacturing firms and financial companies, respectively, had the larger MS units. Management science units located at corporate levels tended to be appreciably larger than those at divisional or other noncorporate levels. The management science units reporting to management information systems or data-processing functions were somewhat larger than those reporting to other administrative or functional groupings.

Incidence of Management Science Units

An investigator soon finds that nearly everyone in business has heard about MS/OR results (usually with at least two apocryphal stories – one about a miraculous solution, the other about a disaster). Hardly anyone, however, can give directions to the MS office or is even sure it exists!

One aspect of this paradox is reflected by the plethora of titles by which such units are known in companies: Only a small fraction of

---

[1] As, for example, the team described by Henry M. Boettinger when he headed MS at AT&T (he is now director of Corporate Planning). This team included experts in statistics, physical sciences, engineering, cost analysis, computer sciences, accounting, mathematics, sociology, psychology, biology, economics, and political science.

Titles containing a combination of the following words, sometimes joined with locally descriptive terms, appeared in a majority of MS/OR unit labels as shown below:

- analysis/analyst/analytical
- data processing
- development
- information
- management
- operations

- planning
- research
- science
- services
- systems
- technical

Still, there are many units in which none of these terms appear: For example, some units simply are called "Special Projects" or are expansively labeled "Capital Administration and Expense Control."

Table 4: Incidence of Management Science Units in Businesses (by principal characteristics)

	Percentage of Firms with MS/OR Units
Type of Business	
Nonmanufacturing	52%
Manufacturing	46
Industrial Average	47
Transportation-Utility	29
Trade-Service	30
Financial	39
Service Average	33
Size of Company	
Large – over 50,000 employees	68
Medium – 10,000 to 49,999 employees	53
Small – under 10,000 employees	33
Census Region	
Northeast	45
North Central	43
South	29
West	48

them go by the unadorned labels "Management Science(s)" or "Operations Research." Although these are the two most frequently reported titles for units defined as MS/OR, some two-thirds of the titles are apparently unique to individual firms.

Such a diversity of titles for units performing a similar function seems hardly accidental, and it aids the impression of MS being everywhere but being invisible. The management scientists themselves prefer to avoid the pompous titles that were sometimes associated with the early MS/OR entrants into business practice.

Estimates of MS/OR units can be only a little more precise than counting the number of angels on the head of a pin because of this vagueness in titles. The summary data in Table 4 appear, however, to represent reasonable estimates of the incidence of MS/OR units in the business sectors (size of firm, type of business, and region) described on page 84.

The nature of MS work, involving as it does substantial data-processing and data-collection resources, makes it likely that such units would occur most frequently in the largest firms. Management science units were more than twice as likely (68 percent) to be found in firms having over 50,000 employees than in

firms having fewer than 10,000 employees (33 percent).

Industrial companies were considerably more likely than service businesses to have MS/OR units. However, within the industrial and service sectors, nonmanufacturing firms (heavily weighted by the presence of oil companies) and financial firms appeared to be especially hospitable to management science activities.

Organizational Setting of Management Science Units

Management science units, like all other company components, can be located within the corporate hierarchy by their positioning at the intersection of several principal coordinates. Of these positioning coordinates, that of *level* – where the unit is situated in the company pyramid (defined by the operational base and the chief executive apex) – and that of *functional context*, the major activity orientation to which it reports directly, are the most commonly used coordinates.

Professional Capital Gains in Homogeneous, "Flow Process" Firms

The evidence is that nonmanufacturing firms – especially oil companies within the industrial sector and financial institutions within the service sector – have the highest rates of MS/OR incidence within their respective business sectors. This confirms a hypothesis suggested by both practitioners and academicians in MS/OR and related fields.

The hypothesis relates the incidence and growth of MS/OR in certain types of businesses to two general propositions: First, it is suggested, MS/OR will spread more rapidly in industries in which companies face a similar set of operating conditions and utilize a similar set of operating technologies. Second, the growth and expansion of MS/OR usage is enhanced if these businesses are characterized by a single basic commodity, one that moves through a flow process by which it (oil, money, raw timber, and so forth) is transformed into a variety of end or intermediate products for, possibly, widely divergent markets.

The hypothesis asserts that in homogeneous, flow-process businesses, professional service units can quickly extend applications from one area of the business to another because of the uniformity of the operating processes, Moreover, innovations in one company tend to be adopted quickly by other firms because of relatively similar environments. In brief, the accumulation and spread of professional capital, in the form of useful experience within both the firm and the business sector, is fairly rapid. This is in contrast to other industries, such as assembly manufacturing, in which individual businesses operate heterogenously and use many different kinds of processes. With assembly industries, observers have noted, there is less opportunity for lessons learned in one end of the business, or in one firm, to be quickly translated into solutions elsewhere.

This should not imply that potential benefits are greater in one type of business sector than another, nor that successes are any less likely in one than another; only that the *diffusion of innovation* will proceed more rapidly in one type of industry than in others.

A slightly different hypothesis that explains the differing incidence of MS/OR units among diverse sectors rests on the level of technological sophistication in given industries. Industries characterized as high-technology (electronics, aerospace, chemicals, and so forth) are, under this theory, expected to accept MS/OR more rapidly than are those operating with more ordinary technology. Evidence exists supporting this theory, which is widely believed by management scientists and their academic counterparts. But it is not always obvious at just what technological level a firm's management feels at home, nor does the evidence uniformly agree with this hypothesis. Some data, at least, convey the impression that a relatively high level of technical competence in a firm can inhibit the establishment of a specialized MS/OR activity since the existing non-MS/OR professionals feel they can absorb and apply MS/OR techniques on their own.

Overall, companies with MS/OR units located at the corporate headquarters level account for almost three-quarters of those studied; the remaining quarter of the units examined operate at divisional or other non-corporate headquarters levels. The following tabulation details the several alternate levels of the management science/operations research units in the companies studied.

Units at *both* corporate and other levels	20%
a) Corp. HQ units 14%	
b) Divisional, other levels 6	
Units *only* at corporate level	59
Units *only* at divisional, other levels	21
	———
	100%

Of firms having MS/OR units at corporate as well as other levels, approximately a third had other MS/OR units reporting directly to the corporate group. The other two-thirds indicated that they had only indirect or "dotted line" reporting relations with other MS units, that is, for functional or technical coordination or for guidance.

These general proportions of MS/OR units located at corporate or divisional or functional levels hold for most companies studied, regardless of size or industry type, within reasonably close tolerances. Two principal exceptions to this pattern occurred, however, neither of which represented a large fraction of the companies studied. Companies that were highly decentralized (i.e., with subsidiaries, affiliates or divisions substantially managed as independent companies in their own right) had less of a concentration of units at headquarters. Here the proportion of corporate-level MS/OR units fell from the average of 75 percent to barely one-half. Secondly, there were companies in the retail-wholesale trade and other miscellaneous service-business sectors where the proportion of corporate-level units rose to over 90 percent.

The Reporting Context

The activity to which MS/OR units report, as contrasted to the level of their positioning, tends to be quite diverse, ranging from "stand-alone" MS units reporting directly to a CEO to MS units that are comingled into another, frequently symbiotic, support or service group (see Table 5, page 36).

Service-Oriented Groupings

Overall, nearly two-fifths of management science units reported to the closely related technical support activities represented by planning, management information systems and data processing, and technical and research service organizations. And over half of these MS units reported to the MIS/DP function in their firms.

The symbiotic link between the technical support activities and MS/OR is related to their complementary specialized functions. These technical activities employ analytical skills that both support and are supported by management science activities. In the MIS/DP case, for example, the capabilities of computer science extend the power of MS applications and are also extended when management scientists introduce new or additional mathematical tools to the computer.

Finance and Accounting Context

In only a slightly different sense, the one-fifth or so of the MS units reporting to organi-

---

"Pure" versus "Mixed" MS/OR Units

Regardless of organizational setting, a majority (60 percent) of the management science units studied stood alone; that is, all of their professional or managerial-level employees worked only on MS projects. Of the remaining 40 percent of the units – in which other professional or managerial specialities were mingled with the management scientists – the largest single category (about a third of the "mixed" units) included management information systems and data processing specialists: computer programmers, systems designers, and the like. The rest of these mixed units contained staff specialists in finance or accounting; marketing (usually marketing research or marketing systems); planning and manufacturing (mostly closely related industrial engineers); research and development (often technical or quantitative methods experts); and other widely assorted staff specialists (public relations, legal, and so forth) in the more heterogeneous general administrative components.

On the average, the mixed units in the survey had almost three times as many other professional-level employees as they did MS specialists. In most cases, too, the average number of MS professionals in these groups was slightly smaller than in "pure" MS units that were otherwise similarly situated (i.e., reporting to the same kind of activity).

Table 5: The Activity Context of Management Science Units by Company Size and Type of Business

Reporting Context	Size of Company — Number of Employees				Type of Business — Industrial			Type of Business — Service			
	Large Over 50,000	Medium 10,000-49,999	Small Less Than 10,000	Total	Non-manufacturing	Manufacturing	Total Industrial	Utility and Transportation	Trade and Service	Financial	Total Service
	Percent of MS Units				Percent of MS Units			Percent of MS Units			
General Administration	13%	22%	38%	26%	11%	25%	23%	23%	38%	37%	32%
Chief Executive Officer	-	5%	19%	9%	4%	10%	9%	15%	6%	3%	8%
General Management (including divisional general management)	7%	9	14	10	4	7	6	8	25	24	19
Administrative Office	6	8	5	7	4	8	8	-	6	9	5
Management Information Systems and Data Processing	28	24	17	22	29	25	25	19	19	9	15
Finance and Accounting Function	23	25	14	21	39	19	22	19	31	12	19
Marketing and/or Manufacturing	6	16	8	12	4	14	12	20	6	6	11
Planning Function	17	7	13	11	7	10	10	16	6	15	13
Technical and Research Service	7	6	6	6	11	5	6	4	-	12	7
All Other	6	-	4	2	-	2	2	4	-	9	4
Total	100%	100%	100%	100%	100%	100%	100%	100%	100%	100%	100%

Note: Details may not add to totals because of rounding.

zations with a financial or accounting context represent a similar arrangement. MS practitioners depend, to a considerable degree, on access to a broad range of accounting-gathered data as inputs to their analyses. By the same token, many of a firm's most important analytical problems arise in, or are assigned to, the financial and accounting activities for study and resolution.[2]

General Administration

Another substantial group of units (just over a quarter overall) report to general or administrative company management, particularly among firms smaller than the very largest. These MS units are responsible to chief execu-

---

[2] It is also fairly common for MIS/DP and planning groups – in many cases, with MS units attached – to report to the financial organization. In the remarks here, however, these MS units report directly to a financial executive to whom MIS/DP or planning units may also report.

tive officers, executive vice presidents, administrative officers, or divisional or functional general management. The proportions of MS units reporting to such general executives grow as the size of the firm declines, with the proportion reporting directly to the chief executive officer rising most dramatically (see Table 5). A third of all MS units among service sector firms report in an administrative context, compared with less than a quarter of the units in the industrial sector.

Firing Line and Other Units

A final grouping of firms place their MS/OR units closer to the operational firing line – principally the marketing or the production and manufacturing organizations. Proportionately, a slightly larger share of these MS units are situated at divisional or other noncorporate levels, often linked as staff to the operating management as part of marketing research or industrial engineering.

Chapter 7
Administrative Issues Affecting Management Science Practice

THE PRINCIPAL administrative issues affecting MS units in business are: (1) those determining how project priorities are set; (2) the related issues of *how*, or even *if*, expected benefits resulting from MS/OR projects are estimated; (3) the absorption of costs – whether or not MS/OR projects are charged to a general overhead account or are charged directly to the organizational component for which they are done; and (4) the degree to which MS units follow up their solutions with practical implementation.

In contrast to the relative formality associated with the mathematical methods used by MS units, these administrative issues, by and large, are dealt with informally, according to most survey participants. Virtually none of them, for example, cited a specific formula for establishing project priorities or benefit cutoff values. Only in regard to cost-allocation procedures were fairly precise rules mentioned by most MS managers, perhaps reflecting more general company allocation policies.

The reasons for this lack of formal rules for administering MS projects are apparent. First of all, many management science projects involve totally new situations, or at least enough novelty so that it is difficult to specify uniform rules. In the larger, multidivisional companies, similar problems will arise sequentially or simultaneously in separate areas of the business, but even here the contextual situation will often be so different as to make the same administrative procedures impractical.

Furthermore, project assignments in MS/OR, almost by definition, carry with them aspects of exploration and thus elements of uncertainty. This uncertainty also discourages prior specification of hard-and-fast procedural policies. Finally, the business situations for which MS assistance is sought are often unstructured and by their very nature defy precise pre-evaluation. Rules for beginning projects and their administrative procedure are often elusive, to say the least. Business searches for new products, for example, have only recently been reduced to a class of decision-making procedures.[1]

This is not to say that MS units have no administrative guidelines for their work. Indeed, almost all MS managers suggested fairly routine and common policies by which they proceed with their work and its applications. It is almost equally evident that these concepts are rarely reduced to rules as exact, or procedures as precise, as the ones MS/OR

[1] E. Patrick McGuire, *Generating New Product Ideas*. The Conference Board, Report No. 546, 1972.

practitioners apply to the decision processes of others.

There does appear to be some firming of procedures as MS groups mature. MS groups that are oldest (established before 1965) or largest (more than eight MS/OR professionals) appear to have more formal, objective criteria for handling projects than do the youngest (established in 1970 or later) or smallest (fewer than three professionals) MS units.

Project Priorities

A third of the MS groups report that the decisions concerning which projects will be undertaken in what order are set by a procedure principally involving general or user management; that is, while MS groups may provide input data (cost and time estimates), the primary decision on priorities lies outside the MS group itself.

While many MS managers answered simply "management" when asked to describe how project priorities were assigned in their unit's practice, others gave more complete descriptions. Several reported essentially political or hierarchical influences: "We assign priorities based on the rank of the requesting officer," to take one example. Others indicate that priorities are assigned according to the "squeaking-wheel rule," or as a result of "client (or user) pressure." Most numerous were those who used phrases such as "management judgment," "management's stated needs," "management-set priorities." Only a small number indicated that formal "steering," "screening," or "management" committees were established to set and review MS project priorities.

A quarter of the MS unit heads reported that priorities were set primarily by the MS unit's own (or its manager's) judgment. "We set priorities based on our judgment of the value of the project," to take one example.

In still other cases, MS management's judgment was exercised within broad guidelines established – and sometimes purposefully altered – by general management. A manager of a divisional MS unit in a major communications company, for instance, reported that priorities were established by MS managers "within guidelines established by our division management. However, the division's management is aware of all ongoing projects and may impute priorities based on importance to top management, corporate concerns, and time and manpower constraints." Sometimes time is the major determinant. A manager of a corporate headquarters unit of a major food processor reports: "Short-term projects having immediate relevance to managerial decisions are given priority."

Another quarter of the MS units reporting described somewhat more formal analyses of project values as the basis for establishing priorities. The most common basis was said to be the "cost of analysis versus probable benefit." This last factor, "probable benefit," corresponds to a technique often associated with MS – the technique of weighting the value of a benefit by the probability of its achievement – a common approach to estimating the expected value of a project.

A major electronics firm's MS unit, located in its research and development organization, described a multifactor priority evaluation: "Projects are selected to match a combination of factors which seek the best overall balance of

(1) Urgency of decision;
(2) Importance of decision;
(3) Capability of MS personnel;
(4) Interest of client;
(5) Mix of short- and long-term considerations; and a
(6) Mix of corporate and divisional interests."

A final group, representing 17 percent of the MS units, simply indicated that MS priorities were set casually, often without specifying who set them. These decisions, one MS manager in a meat packing firm reported, were made "very informally." He noted that a number of factors discouraged "quickie" projects "since the necessity for a more formal system of setting priorities will probably await greater management acceptance of MS.''

Differences in priority-setting procedures seem somewhat related to the age, size and reporting relationship of MS units. For example, the youngest groups appeared somewhat less independent or casual in their priority setting: They report a little less often that they set priorities informally, and they defer to the judgment of their clients or management a little more frequently than do the older units. As noted, the oldest groups mentioned a heavier reliance on objective project-evaluation procedures as a priority-setting guide. These same contrasts are shown in a comparison of smaller and larger MS units.

When MS units are grouped by their principal reporting relationships, the differences in priority-setting procedures are even more marked, perhaps as an indication of the practices of their major functional context. Those units reporting to financial or accounting-oriented management, for example, show a much greater emphasis on user or management judgment in establishing project priorities. MS units that report to general management (including administrative executives), as well as those that report mainly to management information systems and data-processing functions, claim the most reliance on objective estimates of project values as priority guidelines. Those that reported to planning functions are most self-reliant in establishing priorities based on the MS unit's own judgment.

Estimating Benefits

Often one of the most elusive tasks confronting MS units is the estimation of the benefits or contributions that are expected to accrue to the firm's well-being from MS projects or consulting assignments. Clearly, the pragmatic informality of MS administrative procedures and the uncertain, unstructured aspects of MS project work are reasons behind the elusiveness of exact *pre-project benefit* estimates.

An additional source of difficulty, one that affects the measurement of *post-project audits* as well, lies in the sheer dynamics of business. The rapid changes characteristic of business life make it unlikely that conditions at the completion of a project will be the same as at its conception, no matter how short the time span. Indeed, projects aimed at inducing change have their own impact: the mere suggestion of undertaking a project is frequently sufficient to induce spontaneous alteration in the behavior of the business system involved.

By the same token, it is not unknown for MS projects to be undertaken with an initial set of objectives defined by the client and for these to be changed many times before completion. This becomes a sort of Martian baseball, where the bases are shifted after the ball leaves the pitcher's hand.

Other hazards impede the precise auditing of contributions following the successful completion of MS projects. Some of these difficulties arise from the commonly mentioned ''into-the-woodwork'' syndrome: Many decision-making procedures that develop from MS projects become a routine part of the management process; these procedures then meld into the background, a part of day-to-day business normality, losing both their novelty and their identification as MS ''products.'' Often, since the benefits are not measurable until well after the formal completion of the project, actual MS contributions to the company's success diffuse and become difficult to trace and evaluate.

This fading effect is also observable when, as often happens, MS project results are implemented with other changes in business practice. For example, changes in the planning process of an MS project may be introduced simultaneously with changes in the participating personnel. This obscures the independent observation of the effect of these variables on the planning results. Since MS results ultimately depend critically upon the direct or indirect cooperation of others to carry them out, obstacles are raised to the clear-cut attribution of results, either before or after project completion.

These difficulties notwithstanding, efforts were made by a majority of firms represented in this survey to secure project benefit measures, both before initiation and after completion.[2] About three-quarters of the MS managers surveyed indicated that *prior* estimation was accomplished – to some degree, at least – while only a bare majority, reflecting the additional difficulties of *post-project* audits, reported some such effort after project completion.

Who Estimates Pre-Project Benefits?

Of the MS managers who report an effort to establish expected benefits before initiating projects, about a third say that such estimation is attempted jointly by the user-client and the MS unit. Another third report that the user-client alone is responsible for predicting expected benefits.

About a sixth of the MS managers whose firms attempt to predict benefits affirm that the MS unit itself estimates the expected benefits. In this case, the MS unit performs both sides of any cost-benefit ratio prepared for evaluating the proposed project's worth, since the MS unit virtually always is responsible for cost estimation. Finally, about another sixth report that a third party – neither the user-client nor the MS unit – is responsible for estimating benefits expected to accrue from proposed projects. Usually this is an auditing or accounting unit of the company.

While nearly a quarter of MS managers say they have no procedure for (or, in any case, do not do) pre-project benefit estimation, a few of them indicate that benefits are esti-

mated either informally or occasionally (e.g., only for major projects).

Who Audits Post-Project Benefits?

The large increase in MS managers who state that post-project benefits are never – or hardly ever – audited comes primarily from those reporting that their clients, alone or jointly with the MS unit, estimate pre-project benefits. (See Table A-5, Appendix A.) Another sizable group reports that there is no procedure for post-project audits: This report comes from those who indicate the MS unit (or some unspecified unit) does the pre-project benefit estimation. Over half the studied units, however, have their pre- and post-project benefit procedures done in the same way.

Nevertheless, the largest single group performing post-benefit audits consists of those MS units whose clients carry out the measurement. Even so, one MS manager in a power equipment firm suggests that this might be done at the "urging of MS/OR, more often to defend its status than because the client is concerned about cost effectiveness." Some of the MS managers defend the lack of post-project audits by pointing out that many of their projects are ongoing, continuous projects without clear terminal points and, consequently, without an obvious milestone for post-project benefit evaluation.

The largest relative gain in percentage points among those doing post-benefit evaluations was among those participants reporting that a third party (usually an auditing or accounting staff) does the benefit measurement after project completion. In absolute terms, the MS managers who jointly estimate pre-project benefits with their clients note the largest shift away from this procedure in the post-project period. Most reported no post-audit, while others changed to a procedure carried out either by the client or the MS unit alone, or by a third party.

In general, the smallest and youngest MS units (which often, but not always, tend to be the same) seem to have their project benefits estimated *more frequently before* they are

---

[2] MS managers responded to two separate questionings on benefit estimation. In one, these questions were asked: "Do you or does your client have the responsibility of *pre-project benefit* estimation?" "By whom – and how – are benefits evaluated after project completion?" In the other, a question was posed just after identification of the projects through which the participants had made the greatest contribution to the firm. It asked the managers: "By what measure do you evaluate contribution?"

undertaken and less frequently *after* completion. Larger groups, on the other hand, report a somewhat *lower* frequency of *prior* benefit estimation and a *higher* rate of post-project benefit audit. The oldest MS units – again not always identical with the largest ones – are more likely to have some formalized benefit estimation procedures, both before and after undertaking projects, than the average of all MS/OR units.

Measures of Contribution

As noted above (footnote 2) additional information regarding the measure of contribution came from a separate question in which MS managers were asked to discuss the measures used to evaluate the contribution of projects to their firms. The difficulties of making rigorous benefit estimates are confirmed in these managers' comments, and the measures cited offer additional evidence of the obstacles to precise benefit evaluation.

Thus, when describing the measures by which MS contributions to the firm are evaluated, many MS managers use such common indefinite statements as "impact on short- and long-run profits," without clearly specifying how these indexes were developed or formulated. In avoiding discussion of how these measures are derived (or even traced) to MS benefits, the difficulties experienced in accurately identifying either incremental profits or their source seem to be glossed over.

This problem recognized, one of three measures cited by more than a majority of MS managers – *profit impact,* either short or long term – was the most frequently mentioned, alone or in combination with the other two most popular measures. In second place was *user satisfaction.* At best, this is a reflection that the MS project satisfied a client's sense of profitability or cost reduction; at the least, it simply suggests that the client's heart was warmed by the MS effort! The third most frequently mentioned measure was *cost reduction,* the most specific and, perhaps, the easiest (if not always most accurate) measure affecting profitability.

Charge-Back Procedures

Whether or not the serving unit should charge its effort directly to the served unit is usually resolved by company policies on allocating over-head expenses.[3] However, MS unit managers in the survey had their own views and preferences in regard to such policies. Their perspective on this subject, of course, was influenced by the impact of such policies on the acceptance of MS support and accessibility of MS services to user-clients.

The arguments against charge-back procedures usually rest on their inevitable arbitrariness and the consequent bickering with operating management about such things as excessive charges or irrelevant pricing or budgeting decisions. On the other hand, companies that allocate service function costs believe that the additional information and control make the process worthwhile, especially since it keeps both operating and general management aware of service expenses and the need for factoring these costs into their decision making.

Most MS managers indicated that they would be more than satisfied to have their efforts evaluated in terms of MS contributions to the bottom line of their company's profit-and-loss statement. Few, however, are under any illusions about the ease of establishing indisputable profit-contribution measurements. Consequently, to many MS managers the charge-back policy provides a surrogate measure of contribution: The more willing their internal clients are to put up the "dollars" for MS service, the sturdier is the MS unit's reputation for value provided.

There is a second benefit from a policy requiring internal clients to "pay" all or part of MS project costs. The charge-back method

[3] For a discussion of project pricing and charge-back policies in a related area, see "Effects of Pricing and Charge-Back Policies," by John A. Gosden, with comments by others, in *Senior Management and the Data Processing Function.* The Conference Board, Report No. 636, 1974, pp. 63-66. A summary of overhead allocation practices can be found in *How Companies Allocate Corporate Overhead Expenses,* by Paul Macchiaverna, The Conference Board, Information Bulletin No. 17, 1977.

provides an indication of the user's commitment to the MS project. Having to pay for the project reinforces the assurance that the client unit would also provide the involvement and support necessary to the project's success. Finally, some MS practitioners observe that another gain from the direct charge-back of project costs is the ordering of project priorities.

MS unit managers also echo the negative attributes generally associated with charge-back policies. In addition, they point to aspects of such policies that specifically affect MS practice adversely. Many of them express concern about the inhibiting effects on users of mandatory charge-back policies, especially during the early years of an MS function or even later, when the unit was being encouraged to

expand its penetration of new areas. Another inhibiting effect is said to be the discouragement of client support for exploratory research or trial applications, as well as restraining the MS unit from exploring "targets of opportunity" on its own.

Current Practice

Overall, management science groups using some kind of charge-back system for pricing projects to client components outnumber those not using them by about eleven to nine. The most common form is a partial or intermittent system. In a partial charge-back policy, one of two procedures is usually followed: All direct costs – computing costs, outside (the company) charges, extra services outside the MS unit's normal services, and continuing nonstaff costs –

MS Project Implementation

For many years, both MS users and practitioners complained that MS projects resulted in hefty reports that seldom left managers' bookshelves. Users asserted they could not implement MS recommendations for any number of reasons, not the least being that they felt uncertain about practicing what they were not comfortable with. Practitioners were frustrated and sometimes ascribed the lack of implementation of their results to a "lip-service-only" attitude on the part of users.

Current evidence, however, is that implementation is not a serious obstacle to MS acceptance. Three-quarters of all MS units represented in this study appear to be actively engaged in working with their clients to ensure the implementation of successful project results. This activity ranges from carrying out a pilot test to running fully operational tests before turning them over to the client for ongoing use.

In many cases, MS units retain responsibility for maintaining and upgrading the result their work devised for the operating managers in order to keep it serving its objective. In fact, some MS unit managers point out that the

character of their unit's work mix is shifting and creating staffing problems as more professional talent is absorbed in such relatively routine "maintenance" chores.

There is some evidence that implementation efforts on the part of MS teams are related strongly to the results popularly associated with MS activities: Mathematical models tend to be built and put into readiness for operational use by client managers; special-purpose information systems to be carried out in computers, programmed and pilot tested; rules and procedures for analyzing and operating inventory management systems are developed and tested under real conditions; and so on. But, a number of MS practitioners observe that the results of their work can not always be implemented in the ordinary sense by the MS unit, since their efforts often consist of *advice* as to how others might or should act. Actual operating systems, for example, involving significant physical facilities or personnel apparently are less likely to be carried to a "fully operational test" by management scientists than those that involve the MS model or solution process.

are charged to the user. A fractional formula is used in which some of the direct project costs are charged to the client, with the remainder absorbed into an appropriate overhead account. Under policies that charge MS costs to the user only intermittently, a broad range of special cases is covered, the most common denominator of which seems to be the narrowness or uniqueness of the project. Thus, costs of MS projects whose results were seen to be broadly useful were not charged back, while those with only a narrow application were charged to the client.

So-called full charge-back policies reflect a variety of policy alternatives in allocating costs proportionate to usage. Some firms use a form of standard cost formula for allocating project costs to users, with a periodic re-negotiation of the standards. Others report that full costs are recovered only through charges for formal projects. This includes developmental and implementation stages, with charges for exploratory or feasibility phases absorbed in the MS unit's budget (and subsequently by the appropriate overhead account) only if the project goes no further. For the most part, however, full charge-back means just that, or, as several MS managers put it: "Simple. The user pays."

Even among the MS units whose firms have no mandatory charge-back policy, a number of managers report that the user is required to carry the project proposal through a gauntlet of approval steps similar to an investment proposal. In at least one case, an MS manager stated, the client has to make a firm commitment of his own resources to the project, either as a match to the MS unit's costs or as insurance that the client's involvement in the project would be more substantial than just lip service.

Preferred Charge-Back Policies

When asked about their preferences regarding project charge-back practices, two-thirds of the MS managers (only half of whom operated under charge-back policies) indicate their preference for direct charging of full or partial MS project costs to clients. Only a quarter of the MS unit heads believe charging costs to users is undesirable; the remaining managers (fewer than 10) feel that the issue depends on too many factors particular to each unit's individual situation to give a definite opinion.

Most of those who advocate charging project costs to clients, in addition to having cited the value of charge-back policies as surrogate benefit measures, also urge that the MS unit should have some discretionary funds budgeted outside the charge-back policy. These funds would be available for the unit's own research and development, for exploratory studies, for pursuing submerged issues on a contingency basis, and for "free" consulting or assistance to clients who have difficulties that discourage MS participation.

Chapter 8
Management Scientists: Their Preferences

THE DIRECTION in which the practice of management science should go involves certain basic choices. What would the MS managers' preference be for the qualifications of their new recruits? What is considered the most effective position and form for an MS unit in a business organization? The survey results offer some clear opinions on the "ideal" answers to these.

"Ideal" Management Science Recruits

In reporting their preferences for an "ideal" starting-level professional for general MS activities, management science managers chose a different mix of educational qualifications from that represented either by junior or by senior practitioners. The MS managers were also asked to specify a set of prior experience and personal characteristics that they hoped such a candidate would possess.

Formal Educational Qualifications

The MS managers, as a whole, suggested a number of alternative education majors that would satisfy their basic requirements. The largest number of preferences was for candidates whose formal education includes a degree in business administration – the MBA. Frequently, they specified an MBA "with a concentration in quantitative methods." Close behind this is the management sciences group;

in addition to the specialties (management science, operations research, industrial engineering) noted earlier, this area includes systems engineering. At least one degree in business administration *and* the management sciences was preferred by over three-fourths of the MS managers. They are frequently mentioned in tandem: the MBA as a potential key to comprehending management problem situations; and the management science major as a key to problem solving.

Well over half the managers favor a major in mathematics, although many of them seem to be interested primarily in what has been called "mathematical maturity," specifying, for example, "a strong background in math," rather than a formal degree.[1]

Academic training in the "hard" sciences and engineering was mentioned by fewer than half of the managers as a preparation they value highly – and these managers are from the industrial sector or the utility and transportation segment of the service sector. Training in the humanities and social sciences are at

---

[1] Comparing notes with a leading MS practitioner in a Japanese electronics firm finds an even stronger assertion of this tendency. He insists that most Japanese businessmen are wary of hiring individuals whose major has been in "as vague a subject as management science or operations research." They claim that they prefer individuals who have as their main, or at least as their additional, training a major in some specific area of application.

Management Science and Management Development

A number of companies found it profitable to use their management science activity as training ground for selected rising young executives. (For example, see the Standard Oil of California case, Appendix C.) These individuals were usually assigned to the MS unit for one to three years in order to exercise their analytical skills on the problems of other areas of the business.

One company has literally recreated itself through recruiting management science types – mostly MBA's with heavy quantitative majors – who have just taken over management of the business. The principals of this originally family-owned and -operated business decided that they wanted to build their enterprise into an institution that they could take to market (i.e., go public, merge or sell, and, thereby, retrieve their capital).

The family's strategy was relatively simple. Recognizing the need to revitalize and systematize the company's structure and procedures, they engaged in intensive recruiting from the most prestigious, quantitatively oriented graduate schools of business. An initial nucleus of these graduates was then formed into a planning and control arm of the management information-systems function.

Within a relatively few years of pumping carefully selected MBA's through this unit and out into other key staff and operating functions, the entire top echelon of the company was liberally sprinkled with a new type of professional manager new to its experience. This strategy transformed a paternalistically operated business into a more formal, systematically run enterprise whose bottom-line performance quickly brought forth the desired merger – to the satisfaction of the family, its youthful management-science-trained executives, and its new owners, a large consumer-products conglomerate.

The company is now one of the new parent company's best profit-makers. Its executives are frequently called on to aid the parent company in solving new managerial problems and to apply their skills in improving the total corporation's decision-making structure.

---

the bottom of the list, mentioned by fewer than 30 of the managers. And three-fourths of these explicitly mentioned economics or econometrics majors within this category.

Personal Characteristics and Experience

To a large extent, MS managers seem to echo the kinds of experiential or personal qualifications that managers generally look for in new employees, but several differences are notable:

• In the area of work style or attitude, a comment many managers append to this characteristic is the *ability to work alone*, with minimal supervision. This element of solitary initiative stands in marked contrast to more conventional personnel requirements and to what has become a traditional view of MS/OR work as a multidisciplined *team* activity.

• References to *maturity and breadth* seem to reinforce this preference for candidates capable of functioning with relative independence. Comments such as these were common: "all-around background"; "ability to handle oneself well in all kinds of situations"; "knows or is curious about a lot of areas, not restricted to own technology"; "self-starter"; "likes to get things done"; and so forth.

• The candidate's *communications competence* was valued by 43 of the MS managers. While, perhaps, not an unusual requirement in business, it is clearly of special interest in the practice of management science. It is certainly more often sought than found, judging from comments in other business fields and complaints about inarticulate specialists.

• In general, fewer than half the managers looked for prior MS/OR work experience; just over a quarter want prior business experience, with most of them desiring experience in the same kind of industry rather than in a general business background.

Implications for Future Training

There is considerable evidence, both from the observations cited and from frequent discussions in both MS/OR literature and in general business publications, that the prospective management scientist would be well advised to acquire a double-barreled set of qualifications. And it is not surprising that no single curriculum seems to exist to supply them both with equal effectiveness.

On the one hand, individuals looking forward to practicing in this field must have a firm grasp of their tool-kit fundamentals, one ensuring proficiency with the mathematical implements of MS/OR. In this connection, many management scientists decry the so-called cookbook approach so often used to teach students the basic MS/OR techniques, which leaves them without the knowledge necessary for flexible and self-confident application in actual practice.

Some management science consultants assert that they are beginning to sense a slight movement away from concentrations on educational majors like management science – with its primary emphasis on analytical methodology – toward fields that emphasize instead knowledge in the substantive areas to which the methods are applied. The chief executive of a leading management-science consulting firm, for example, reports that professionals who have had either basic or additional training in a field of theory – like economics – seem to have superior problem-defining competencies and are more effective at getting to the heart of obscure, unstructured problems.

And, as many practitioners note, what must be learned about how businesses actually run is difficult to acquire formally. Some educators in the MS field are already experimenting with the equivalent of "laboratory" courses in which students work on real problems, either as "interns" in businesses or other institutions, or as "campus management scientists,"

acquiring practice in finding, studying and developing MS solutions.

"Ideal" Management Science Unit Positioning

Where would MS/OR managers prefer their units to be positioned for maximum effectiveness? In sharing their thoughts on "ideal" positioning, the study participants for the most part disregarded their unit's current company location.

Their answers fall, roughly, into four principal categories. Two of the categories correspond to the level and functional contexts, discussed earlier, although expressed in somewhat less precise terms; a third refers mostly to several variations on the form an MS unit might take. A fourth category brings together a number of different ways of saying "it doesn't make much difference." One example of this attitude is the successful MS manager of a financial institution who says: "Look, it doesn't really matter where or to whom we report as long as it's a sufficiently sympathetic situation – the boss's title doesn't matter, his compatibility with us does."

Many of the MS managers reflect this attitude in their responses, hinting at a specific reporting context rather than stating it. Certainly, few of the MS managers insist on reporting "directly to the chief executive officer" – a positioning thought to be a sine qua non in the early years of MS penetration into business.

The Level

Most of the managers who explicitly mention a level favor a central MS unit at corporate headquarters, usually with other units (or individuals) assigned to areas of the company where an ongoing need for MS work exists. In this arrangement, the corporate unit would perform the customary headquarters services, as reflected in current practice – supporting general management, corporate planning, corporate financial modeling, and so forth – with at least functional surveillance responsibilities over the subsidiary units or individuals.

According to the recommendations of some participants, the corporate unit would constitute a corporate cadre that would do the MS research and development required, would provide top professional support to the subsidiary units or individuals, and, only in special cases, would handle particularly difficult, complex or far-reaching problems that were beyond the other practitioners' capacity. Essentially, it would function as a central resource and a backup for the dispersed units. While some managers note that the company's size is a factor in supporting so well-articulated an MS function, others comment that the use of individual MS *practitioners* at the subsidiary levels rather than MS *groups,* perhaps on a rotating assignment basis, enable the company-size restriction to be mitigated.

Still another group of MS managers, however, favors placing MS units only in corporate headquarters. And a few others prefer placing such groups only at the divisional level. These mentions, explicitly stating a preferred level, totaled fewer than 30 percent of all the "ideal" recommendations. Another group, about half as large, simply implied a level: "The unit should be high up in the company" – to take one example.

The Reporting Context

The most explicit comments by MS managers referred to the reporting context that they prefer for their units. About 34 percent of the mentions specify the following reporting preferences: The general management group (including CEO, general executives, administrative executives, division general management and executive, senior, or top vice-president) comprises well over half of the explicit mentions. The remaining mentions are fairly evenly divided among those that prefer a reporting relationship with the planning function, the MIS/DP department, finance, research and development, or some "traditional function."

The "Ideal" Form of an MS Unit

Over a quarter of the mentions include some discussion of the form an MS unit should take. Most often volunteered is the notion of a "completely separate group" (i.e., a unit not embedded within another functional unit like MIS/DP or planning). Usually, MS managers urging separateness prefer reporting directly to general management.

In this topic of ideal form, those managers who urge adoption of the corporate-cadre form are included. Additionally, a smaller group of managers favors the complete dispersion of MS units as such, with individual management scientists being assigned to whatever company components need, or can use, their services. These individuals would assume the normal responsibilities of members of the component to which they were assigned (as marketers, factory management, planners).

A few MS managers mentioned that ideal MS units should be made up of individuals assigned for a fixed period on a rotational basis, who subsequently return to other functions for their continuing careers.

Chapter 9
The Future of Management Science

DESPITE A RECORD of continuing successful applications, as well as an expanding list of projects in the strategic areas of top management interest, MS/OR professionals in the study express concern about their future role in business.

One of the reasons for their disquiet is the alacrity with which professionals in other fields absorb and apply the very tools management scientists have for so long considered their own. Industrial engineers, computer professionals, accountants, financial experts, "hard" engineers and scientists, newly minted MBA's, and a whole host of specialists have acquired many of the skills that were once the unique possession of management scientists.

Given this proliferation of business recruits who have other, more traditionally acceptable, business skills, management scientists may well wonder who will be doing their work in the years to come. Some already argue for the absorption of their "profession" by the managers with the problems. Related to this is the tendency, noted earlier, of MS products "to disappear into the woodwork" – the phenomenon of successful MS procedures becoming so accepted and so routinely applied that the users forget the source. To be effective as advisers and problem solvers to management, management scientists, like other staff experts, must make sure the client gets the credit for the MS unit's successes while

they retain a clear responsibility for MS failures.

"What have you done for us lately?" This is, therefore, a question MS managers often find difficult to answer, despite the volume of successes they turn over to users. It seems futile to inquire why this should be so, why the identity of the special MS content in problem solutions tends to disappear while, for example, double-entry bookkeeping is still, after centuries, recognized as a proprietary function of the accounting profession. Most management scientists accept the disappearance of their best results into the corporate woodwork as inevitable, another one of the factors that makes their work so difficult to evaluate at the bottom line.

Quite different groups of management scientists interviewed appear impervious to any concern about the "everywhere-nowhere" paradox of MS/OR. One group consists of older, more experienced practitioners, often MS managers, with a healthy capital of successful and well-accepted personal practice among their management clientele. These older hands, with visible individual track records, enjoy status and accessibility to senior management and are probably as secure as any senior staff specialists in business could hope to be. The other group untroubled by the dilemma of MS's future consists mainly of younger specialists, also including managers, who regard MS practice as a stepping stone, perhaps even a key one, to advancement into other, more rewarding opportunities in business.

In the end, the question of MS/OR's future as a separate and specialized business activity may rest on just how clearly differentiated the profession is from other business professions or occupational categories.[1] A typical evolutionary cycle of a profession starts, for example, with a particular body of knowledge that is developed and extended by a research and development branch (usually in academia), which trains future researchers (academicians) as its own source of replacements. This branch prepares and qualifies practitioners for applying the body of knowledge in those contexts for which it has effective applicability. Ideally, the cycle should be constantly regenerated by the practitioners and by others in the field (users or researchers in allied areas) who discover the anomalies of the received information through experience and application.

While the domain of management science can be identified in terms of the problems MS

practitioners work on, many professionals perceive that it is a shifting definition at best. Many of the MS managers surveyed recognize that their domain has a strong overlap, in the minds of business people, with those of other managers in the operating and support functions of business. These managers, after all, are also problem solvers in their own bailiwicks. If, in addition, they have, or can acquire, the skills of the MS/OR specialists, what happens to the domain identified as that of management science?

The professional careerists in MS/OR may be superseded by more generally trained managers with MS training, thereby destroying the self-regenerating professional cycle described earlier, dependent as it is on the mutual stimulation between the MS academic and the MS practitioner. Some have argued that the existence of a self-regenerating "critical mass" of both theoretical and applied professionals talking the same "language," is vital to sustain management science as a valuable management resource.

In general, though, this appears not to be an issue which the management scientists, applied or theoretical, can usefully answer by themselves. The answer must come from their employers – be they the corporate executives who approve the budgets or the managers who use MS services. If the future is to include a self-regenerating "critical mass" of academics and field professionals, it appears that MS/OR practitioners may require a more carefully designed organizational setting, one that provides both the stability and the recognition of an established specialty. If not, then some thought must be given to how – and by whom – this particular wheel will be reinvented (and reintegrated into the management process) when it is needed in the succeeding generations of management problems.

---

[1] "A profession has three generally accepted attributes: (1) It involves essentially intellectual activity after long, specialized, education and training. (2) It is service oriented, placing that aim before personal gain. (3) It sets its own standards, adopts a code of ethics, and has a strong, closely knit professional organization." Eileen B. Hoffman, *Unionization of Professional Societies*. The Conference Board, Report No. 690 1976, p. 1. Two federal statutes are crucial in defining a "professional" because of the rights conferred or removed by law from professional occupations. Under the 1938 Fair Labor Standards Act (also known as the Wage and Hour Law), *professional administrative* and *managerial* employees meeting certain minimal earnings and job criteria are exempt from the receipt of premium pay. Computer programmers, systems analysts, management science/operations research analysts, and journalists, among others, seem not to have been included in the *professional* category.

The other law, the Labor-Management Relations (Taft-Hartley) Act of 1947, defines professional employees, in the course of delimiting bargaining units, in a manner requiring case-by-case adjudication for its applicability to specific occupations. No case involving management scientists/operations researchers has come to this author's attention.

Appendixes

Appendix A
Supplemental Survey Tables

Table A-1: Management Science Projects Making the Greatest Contributions and Receiving the Most Attention

Project Application Areas	Making the Greatest Contribution to the Firm		Receiving the Most MS Unit Attention	
	Number	Percent	Number	Percent
Financial Applications				
Accounting systems	9	1.4%	15	2.1%
Budgeting and control	18	2.9	7	1.0
Capital budgeting	10	1.6	21	3.0
Cash flow analysis	13	2.1	17	2.4
Credit analysis	1	0.2	1	0.1
Currency exchange	1	0.2	1	0.1
Financial information systems	19	3.1	23	3.2
Investment analysis	16	2.6	19	2.7
Long-range financial forecasting	12	1.9	14	2.0
Merger/acquisition financing	4	0.6	3	0.4
Portfolio analysis	13	2.1	12	1.7
Risk/venture analysis	18	2.9	23	3.2
Tax incidence analysis	7	1.1	7	1.0
Transfer pricing	1	0.2	3	0.4
General Management Applications				
Acquisition/merger analysis	3	0.5	4	0.6
Corporate planning models	37	6.0	41	5.8
Designing planning process	8	1.3	7	1.0
Developing plans	6	1.0	7	1.0
Environmental impact studies	1	0.2	1	0.1
Facilities planning	29	4.7	26	3.7
Generating strategy alternatives	4	0.6	4	0.6
General management information systems	6	1.0	11	1.6
Goal determination	–	–	–	–
Long-range economic forecasting	19	3.1	24	3.4
Long-range technological forecasting	6	1.0	7	1.0
Objectives determination	1	0.2	1	0.1
Strategy evaluation	2	0.3	4	0.6

Table A-1: Management Science Projects Making the Greatest Contributions and Receiving the Most Attention (continued)

Project Application Areas	Making the Greatest Contribution to the Firm		Receiving the Most MS Unit Attention	
	Number	Percent	Number	Percent
Logistics Applications				
Distribution information systems	6	1.0	6	0.8
Inventory management	29	4.7	37	5.2
Physical distribution	17	2.8	20	2.8
Storage/distribution facility planning	13	2.1	16	2.3
Transport management	7	1.1	9	1.3
Personnel Applications				
Benefit analysis	3	0.5	4	0.6
Employee records	–	–	–	–
Government regulations compliance	4	0.6	4	0.6
Labor relations	–	–	–	–
Manpower forecasting	9	1.4	10	1.4
Organization development	1	0.2	1	0.6
Personnel development	–	–	–	–
Personnel information systems	4	0.6	7	1.0
Personnel selection programs	–	–	–	–
Productivity analysis	7	1.1	6	0.8
Time and methods analysis	2	0.3	1	0.1
Wage/salary analysis	1	0.2	–	–
Production Management Area				
Batch process control	1	0.2	1	0.1
Computerized machine or process control	3	0.5	5	0.7
Flow process control	3	0.5	3	0.4
Job design	–	–	–	–
Plant or process layout or sequencing	3	0.5	3	0.4
Production methods research	26	4.2	27	3.8
Production information systems	4	0.6	4	0.6
Production planning	41	6.9	43	6.1
Production scheduling	14	2.3	17	2.4
Production sequencing	1	0.2	1	0.1
Purchasing control	10	1.6	9	1.3
Quality control	6	1.0	8	1.1
Sales/Marketing Applications				
Advertising management	4	0.6	3	0.4
Competitive analysis	2	0.3	2	0.3
Competitive bidding situations	4	0.6	5	0.7
Marketing information systems	9	1.4	12	1.7
Marketing strategy analysis	15	2.4	15	2.1
Marketing research	28	4.5	39	5.5
New product analysis	12	1.9	13	1.8
Product life cycle analysis	2	0.3	2	0.3
Pricing studies	18	2.9	21	3.0
Product or line strategy	10	1.6	11	1.6
Sales territory analysis	4	0.6	6	0.8
Other Applications	17	2.8	19	2.7

Table A-2: Popularity of Major Management Science Application Areas and Projects in Business

Project Application Areas	Engaged in Past Five Years		Actively Engaged in Now[1]		Expect to Engage in Next Few Years	
	Number	Percent	Number	Percent	Number	Percent
Financial Applications						
Accounting systems	59	34%	37	21%	43	25%
Budgeting and control	70	40	59	34	72	42
Capital budgeting	87	49	67	38	87	50
Cash flow analysis	109	62	81	46	109	63
Credit analysis	28	16	14	8	21	12
Currency exchange	20	11	16	9	27	16
Financial information systems	76	43	65	37	79	46
Investment analysis	83	47	67	38	78	45
Long-range financial forecasting	82	46	77	44	99	57
Merger/acquisition financing	36	20	16	9	35	20
Portfolio analysis	30	17	19	11	37	21
Risk/venture analysis	67	38	39	22	77	44
Tax incidence analysis	21	12	10	6	18	10
Transfer pricing	26	15	15	9	27	16
Net Financial Applications	**161**	**92**	**147**	**86**	**154**	**91**
General Management Applications						
Acquisition/merger analysis	45	26	22	13	50	29
Corporate planning models	110	62	98	56	127	73
Designing planning process	48	27	36	21	50	29
Developing plans	57	32	55	31	63	36
Environmental impact studies	22	12	13	7	24	14
Facilities planning	87	49	60	34	85	49
Generating strategy alternatives	60	34	62	35	82	47
General management information systems	68	39	59	34	73	42
Goal determination	24	14	28	16	43	25
Long-range economic forecasting	70	40	70	40	91	53
Long-range technological forecasting	23	13	15	9	37	21
Objectives determination	19	11	23	13	32	18
Strategy evaluation	53	30	52	30	73	42
Net General Management Applications	**163**	**94**	**157**	**91**	**160**	**94**
Logistics Applications						
Distribution information systems	61	35	41	23	57	32
Inventory management	88	50	72	41	84	49
Physical distribution	62	35	37	21	53	31
Storage/distribution facility planning	61	35	33	19	55	32
Transport management	36	20	18	10	42	24
Net Logistics Applications	**112**	**64**	**94**	**55**	**112**	**66**
Personnel Applications						
Benefit analysis	37	21	19	11	30	17
Employee records	21	12	16	9	17	10
Government regulations compliance	18	10	15	9	22	13

Table A-2: Popularity of Major Management Science Application Areas and Projects in Business (continued)

Project Application Areas	Engaged in Past Five Years		Actively Engaged in Now[1]		Expect to Engage in Next Few Years	
	Number	Percent	Number	Percent	Number	Percent
Labor relations	14	8	10	6	12	7
Manpower forecasting	39	22	27	15	49	28
Organization development	18	10	10	6	21	12
Personnel development	12	7	9	5	12	7
Personnel information systems	27	15	21	12	29	17
Personnel selection programs	12	7	5	3	11	6
Productivity analysis	38	22	27	15	44	25
Time and methods analysis	19	11	17	10	20	12
Wage/salary analysis	30	17	15	9	31	18
Net Personnel Applications	**97**	**56**	**73**	**42**	**96**	**57**
Production Management Area						
Batch process control	20	11	20	11	27	16
Computerized machine or process control	27	15	24	14	32	18
Flow process control	18	10	9	5	14	8
Job design	7	4	7	4	8	5
Plant or process layout or sequencing	29	17	24	14	27	16
Production methods research	18	10	17	10	18	10
Production information systems	39	22	36	21	40	23
Production planning	74	42	69	39	81	47
Production scheduling	71	40	59	34	77	44
Production sequencing	25	14	22	13	33	19
Purchasing control	21	12	17	10	25	14
Quality control	32	18	23	13	27	16
Net Production Applications	**103**	**59**	**103**	**60**	**110**	**65**
Sales/Marketing Applications						
Advertising management	19	11	12	7	23	13
Competitive analysis	47	27	41	23	48	28
Competitive bidding situations	31	18	17	10	24	14
Marketing information systems	56	32	48	27	58	34
Marketing strategy analysis	54	31	48	27	61	35
Marketing research	72	41	58	33	71	41
New product analysis	46	26	30	17	46	27
Product life cycle analysis	33	19	24	14	48	28
Pricing studies	72	41	52	30	67	39
Product or line strategy	34	19	31	18	46	27
Sales territory analysis	34	19	26	15	37	21
Net Sales/Marketing Applications	**128**	**74**	**115**	**67**	**125**	**74**
Other Applications	5	3	6	3	6	3

[1] Last half of 1975.

Table A-3: Educational Background of Management Practitioners (excluding management science unit heads)

Major Fields	Overall Total		Juniors[1]		Seniors[1]	
	Number	Percent*	Number	Percent*	Number	Percent*
Single Fields of Concentration						
Mathematical Sciences	142	19%	98	24%	44	13%
Engineering and Science	126	17	49	12	77	24
Business Curricula	117	16	66	16	51	16
Management Sciences	87	12	50	12	37	11
Social Sciences and Humanities	46	6	24	6	22	7
Subtotal	518	70	287	69	231	71
Multiple Fields[2]						
Management Sciences *Plus:*[2]						
Mathematical Sciences	39	5	20	5	19	6
Engineering and Science	36	5	18	4	18	6
Business Curricula	34	5	21	5	13	4
Social Sciences and Humanities	9	1	3	1	6	2
Subtotal	118	16	62	15	56	17
Business Curricula *Plus:*[2]						
Engineering and Science	29	4	18	4	11	3
Social Sciences and Humanities	24	3	14	3	10	3
Mathematical Sciences	22	3	18	4	4	1
Subtotal	75	10	50	12	25	8
Engineering and Science *Plus:*[2]						
Mathematical Sciences	19	3	9	2	10	3
Social Sciences and Humanities	5	1	3	1	2	1
Subtotal	24	3	12	3	12	4
Mathematical Sciences *Plus:*[2]						
Social Sciences and Humanities	8	1	5	1	3	1
Overall Total	743	100%	416	100%	327	100%

* Details may not add to totals or subtotals because of rounding.

[1] "Juniors" and "Seniors" in this table represent an arbitrary classification based, respectively, on 1975 annual base salaries *under* and *equal to or over* $25,000.

[2] Each of the multiple fields of concentration can be read in either direction, that is, the 39 MS practitioners with majors in Management Sciences *plus* Mathematical Sciences could be reported as having majors in Mathematical Sciences *plus* Management Sciences; sequence of majors was not preserved in the original reported data. For editorial simplicity this table is constructed only of the unduplicated listings taken in order of the frequency of the aggregates of the initial major listed – that is, the *most* multiple listings included Management Sciences, the *least* included Social Sciences and Humanities. The full table, including duplications, can be constructed from the data shown.

Table A-4: Size of Management Science Units by Various Characteristics[1]

Characteristics	Number of Full-time MS/OR Professionals			
	Average Number	Median Number	Inter-Quartile Range	Overall Range
Total – All Units	6	4	2 – 7	1 – 31
Size of Company				
Large – over 50,000 employees	9	8	3 – 14	1 – 31
Medium – 10,000 – 49,999 employees	6	4	3 – 7	1 – 23
Small – under 10,000 employees	5	3	2 – 5	1 – 18
Type of Business				
Industrial	6	4	2 – 8	1 – 31
Nonmanufacturing	9	5	3 – 15	1 – 31
Manufacturing	6	3	2 – 7	1 – 23
Service	5	4	2 – 6	1 – 18
Financial	6	4	2 – 11	1 – 18
Nonfinancial	5	5	3 – 7	1 – 17
Age of Unit				
Young – begun since 1969	3	3	2 – 4	1 – 9
Medium – begun 1965-1969	5	3	2 – 7	1 – 23
Old – begun before 1965	9	6	3 – 15	1 – 31
Locational Level of Unit				
Corporate Level	7	4	3 – 9	1 – 31
Noncorporate Level	4	3	2 – 5	1 – 17
Reporting Context of Unit				
Management Information Systems/Data Processing	8	4	3 – 14	1 – 31
Finance/Accounting	5	3	2 – 5	1 – 20
General Management/Administrative	6	5	2 – 8	1 – 23
Marketing/Manufacturing	6	5	3 – 7	1 – 19
Planning	6	3	2 – 6	1 – 23

[1] Size of unit is measured by number of full-time MS/OR professionals only.

Table A-5: Who Does Pre- or Post-Project Benefit Estimations?[1]

Pre-Project Benefit Estimation	Post-Project Benefit Estimation														Pre-Project Total	
	Rarely Done		Only Done in Special Cases		Jointly by Client and MS Unit		Done by Client Unit		Done by MS/OR Unit		Done by Third Party		Done, but Unspecified by Whom[2]			
	Number	Percent	Number	Percent	Number	Percent	Number	Percent	Number	Percent	Number	Percent	Number	Percent	Number	Percent
Rarely done	**52**	**25%**	–	–	–	–	1	*	2	1%	1	*	1	*	57	28%
Only done in special cases	1	*	**3**	**2%**	1	*	–	–	–	–	–	–	–	–	5	2
Jointly by client and MS unit	12	6	3	2	**22**	**11%**	9	4%	4	2	6	3%	–	–	56	27
Done by client/user	11	5	2	1	2	1	**21**	**10**	3	2	4	2	1	*	44	21
Done by MS/OR unit	6	3	–	–	1	*	4	2	**9**	**4**	2	1	–	–	22	11
Done by third party	–	–	–	–	–	–	–	–	–	–	**1**	*	–	–	1	*
Done, but unspecified	7	3	–	–	1	*	–	–	–	–	–	–	**12**	**6%**	20	10
Post-Project Total	89	43%	8	4%	27	13%	35	17%	18	9%	14	7%	14	7%	205	100% 80%

	Number	Percent
No Answer: Before or After	27	11
No Answer: Before	2	1
No Answer: After	21	8
Total:	255	100%

* Less than 1 percent after rounding. Details may not add to totals because of rounding.
[1] Numbers and percentages in bold-faced type indicate same benefit estimation procedure followed in both pre- and post-project.
[2] While benefit estimation was described, response did not indicate by whom it was done.

Relations with Other Staffs

To complete the picture of MS/OR relationships within their companies, managers of MS units were asked to express their opinions about the other service or staff units in their firms with which it is most important that the MS/OR unit maintain close working relations.[1] Five such units were cited to the MS managers as examples of units that might be important for the MS/OR unit to keep close ties with: management information systems/data processing, controller's office, corporate or divisional planning group, marketing research, and manufacturing engineering.

[1] The exact question asked MS/OR managers was this: "In your opinion, with what *other service or staff units* in your company (for example, information systems, or data processing, controller's office, corporate or divisional planning group, market research, manufacturing engineering, et cetera) is it most important that MS/OR maintain close working relations? Please discuss why." (Emphasis added.)

In looking at Table A-6, the following points ought to be kept in mind:

• While most MS units report to one or another of the five major reporting contexts listed across the top of the table, their comments on units considered important to maintain close working relations with seem *not* to be influenced by their reporting relationship.

• A majority of the MS managers' comments mention one or more of these five units, and one-third of the managers mention *all five*.

• "All other mentions" includes R and D units, other engineering units, and other MS/OR units in the company.

• A number of MS managers, 14 percent, surpass the intent of the question and insist that their *user-clients*, not necessarily service or support units, are the most important ones to foster close relations with.

Table A-6: Other Staff Units Considered by Management Science Managers to Be Important for Close Working Relations

| | Major Reporting Context | | | | | | | | | | | |
| Other Major Service or Support Areas | Management Information Systems/Data Processing | | Finance/Accounting | | General Administration | | Marketing/Manufacturing | | Planning | | Total* | |
	Number	Percent	Number	Percent	Number	Percent	Number	Percent	Number	Percent	Number	Percent
Management Information Systems/Data Processing	22	22%	18	20%	18	19%	17	19%	8	16%	83	19%
Planning Groups	15	15	14	16	10	10	13	14	11	22	63	15
Financial/Accounting	13	13	13	14	15	16	15	16	7	14	63	15
Marketing Research/Other Marketing Units	7	7	5	6	8	8	9	10	4	8	33	8
Manufacturing Engineering/Other Manufacturing	3	3	5	6	5	5	10	11	2	4	25	6
All Five of Above	17	17	17	19	20	21	17	19	11	22	82	19
User-Client Components	15	15	15	17	13	14	9	10	7	14	59	14
All Other Mentions	7	8	3	3	6	5	1	1	1	2	18	4
Total mentions = Base =	99		90		95		91		51		426	100%
Managers reporting = 228												

* The All Other reporting context group, accounting for less than 2 percent of the responses, is omitted.

Appendix B
Management Science Techniques and Usage in Business

THE FOLLOWING definitions of the most common management science techniques and the references to literature where they are discussed in detail have been selected and adapted from *A Dictionary* *for Marketing Research,* edited by Irving Roshwalb and published by Audits Surveys, Inc., of New York, N.Y., 1974, with permission.

ANALYSIS OF VARIANCE

Techniques that assess different sources' contributions to the overall variability of data.

A.M. Mood, *Introduction to Statistical Method.* New York, N.Y.: McGraw-Hill Book Company, 1957.

BAYESIAN (ANALYSIS) INFERENCE

A form of decision-making that involves the use of subjective (personalistic) estimates of the probabilities of certain events in evaluating the "expected return" of an alternative.

(See Subjective Probability under the "Probability" definition)

R. Schlaifer, *Probability and Statistics for Business Decisions.* New York, N.Y.: McGraw-Hill Book Company, 1959.

CLUSTER (ANALYSIS)

In "Data Analysis" a set of similar objects (or ideas), where similarity can be defined: for example, in terms of homogeneity of objects within a cluster. The purpose of such analysis is to reduce the information content of many items to a description of the few central ideas contained in them.

R.C. Tryon and D.E. Bailey, *Cluster Analysis.* New York, N.Y.: McGraw-Hill Book Company, 1970.

COMPUTER SIMULATION (See "Operational Gaming")

CONSUMER BEHAVIOR

A mathematical description of the activities of the individual as those activities relate to the shopping for, and purchase of, consumer items.

T.S. Robertson, *Consumer Behavior.* Glenview, Ill.: Scott, Foresman & Company, 1970.

CRITICAL PATH METHOD (CPM) (/ PERT)

In a complex operation, made up of many smaller but interrelated steps, the time required to complete the entire operation is equal to the most time-consuming path one can find from the start to the finish of the entire operation. This path is known as the Critical Path.

(See also "Program Evaluation Review Technique")

W.R. King, *Quantitative Analyses for Marketing Management*. New York, N.Y.: McGraw-Hill Book Company, 1967.

DECISION TREE (ANALYSIS)

The decision tree is a visual device for depicting decision options and the consequences of particular decisions in terms of the probability of a given event occurring.

H. Raiffa, *Decision Analysis: Introductory Lectures on Choices Under Uncertainty*. Reading, Mass.: Addison-Wesley Publishing Company, 1968.

DESIGN OF EXPERIMENTS (See "Experimental Design")

DYNAMIC PROGRAMMING

A technique for determing the optimal return from a plan of sequential decisions over a known period of time.

R.S. Ledley, *Programming and Utilizing Digital Computers*. New York, N.Y.: McGraw-Hill Book Company, 1962.

EXPERIMENTAL DESIGN

Procedures that provide data to permit valid judgments to be made regarding the relative value of various designated alternatives.

A.L. Edwards, *Experimental Design in Psychological Research*. New York, N.Y.: Holt, Rinehart & Winston, 1960.
S. Banks, *Experimentation in Marketing*. New York, N.Y.: MGraw-Hill Book Company, 1965.

FACTOR ANALYSIS

The purpose of factor analysis is to examine the joint observations on a large number of variables in order to determine and measure the existence of a smaller number of key factors which can reconstruct the original observations.

H.H. Harman, *Modern Factor Analysis*. Chicago, Ill.: University of Chicago Press, 1967.

GAME THEORY

A method of studying and analyzing opposing strategies to determine the "best" strategy.

J. Von Neumann, O. Morgenstern, *Theory of Games and Economic Behavior*. New York, N.Y.: John Wiley & Sons, 1964.

HEURISTIC (METHODS) PROGRAMMING

A system of solution which involves a trial and error investigation of the various alternatives until a feasible solution is found.

INFORMATION THEORY

As developed by Shannon, information deals with the capacity of a communication channel – that is, the ability to transmit what is produced out of a source of information.

C.E. Shannon, W. Weaver, *The Mathematical Theory of Communications*. Urbana, Ill.: The University of Illinois Press, 1949.

H. Quastler, *Information Theory in Psychology — Problems and Methods*. Glencoe, Ill.: The Free Press, 1955.

INTEGER PROGRAMMING

Integer Programming deals with the class of optimization problems in which some or all of the variables are required to be integers.

M.L. Balinski, "Integer Programming: Methods, Uses and Computation," *Management Science,* November, 1965.

LINEAR PROGRAMMING

Programming problems are concerned with the efficient use, or allocation of, limited resources to meet desired objectives. The problem is to choose from many solutions the one (optimal) that best meets the objectives within the conditions specified.

Linear Programming problems are a special case of programming problems which employ a mathematical model or description of the problem involving relationships which are straight-line or linear.

(See Nonlinear Programming)

A.M. Glicksman, *Linear Programming and Theory of Games*. New York, N.Y.: John Wiley & Sons, 1963.

F. Dorfman, P.A. Samuelson, R.W. Solov, *Linear Programing and Economic Analysis*. New York, N.Y.: McGraw-Hill Book Company, 1958.

MAPPING (See "Perceptual Mapping")

MULTIVARIATE ANALYSIS (TECHNIQUES)

Techniques that deal with the simultaneous consideration of several variables. Simple and Multiple regression techniques are examples, as are factor analysis, cluster analysis and discriminant analysis.

M.G. Kendall, *A Course in Multivariate Analysis*, London, England: Methuen Publishing Company, 1961.

W.W. Cooley and P.R. Lohnes, *Multivariate Procedures for Behavioral Sciences*. New York, N.Y.: John Wiley & Sons, 1962.

NONLINEAR PROGRAMMING

A variant of linear programming that does not require that the incremental value of each resource in a given application remain constant as more of the resource is used.

Nonlinearity describes a relationship between, say, two variables in which a unit change in one variable does not always imply a constant change in the other.

C. Emory, P. Niland, *Making Management Decisions*. Boston, Mass.: Houghton-Mifflin Co., 1968.

OPERATIONAL GAMING (Example of Simulation)

Used to train personnel in management procedures. Computer is used to keep track of decisions – and their consequences – of teams operating competing firms in an industry.

P.S. Greenwall, L.W. Herron, R.H. Rawdon, *Business Simulation in Industrial and University Education*. Englewood Cliffs, N.J.: Prentice-Hall, Inc., 1962.

PERCEPTUAL MAPPING

A geometric representation of the attributes of an object (e.g., a brand of a product) as viewed by the respondents. Gaps between "maps" of different brands and the ideal product may indicate areas for new product development.

PROBABILITY (THEORY)

A measure of the likelihood that a given event will occur. There are two approaches to the determination of this measure:

Objective probability – the probability that the event will occur in a single trial is the ratio of that event's occurrence in a series of experiments. Also known as the "frequency theory of probability."

Subjective probability – the probability that an event will occur is one's personal (subjective) degree of belief in its occurrence.

R. Von Mises, *Probability, Statistics and Truth*, 2nd. ed. rev. London, England: Allen & Unwin, 1961.
W. Weaver, *Lady Luck, The Theory of Probability*. Garden City, N.Y.: Doubleday & Company, 1963.

PROGRAM EVALUATION REVIEW TECHNIQUE (PERT)

A method of planning and evaluating progress of a complex effort so that its objectives will be accomplished on time. A major benefit of this technique is that it provides a diagram of the entire operation and offers the opportunity for examining possible trade-offs among different elements of the operation. CPM is used along with PERT to indicate the likely time of completion of the entire project.

(See Critical Path Method)

QUEUEING, QUEUEING THEORY, QUEUEING ANALYSIS

Deals with a class of problems, and the procedures for their solution, that have as their main concern the possibility of many users requiring service from a limited number of suppliers. Simply, the provision of a service that minimizes the customers' waiting time.

D.R. Cox and W.L. Smith, *Queues*. New York, N.Y.: John Wiley & Sons, 1961.

REGRESSION ANALYSIS

Statistical techniques that measure the degree to which variables are related. In regression analysis the researcher uses his knowledge of what is called an "independent variable" (e.g., advertising) to determine the magnitude of a "dependent variable" (e.g., sales). This class of techniques includes correlation analysis.

J. Griffin, *Statistics: Methods and Applications.* New York, N.Y.: Holt, Rinehart & Winston, 1962. M. Ezekiel and K.A. Fox, *Methods of Correlation and Regression Analysis.* New York, N.Y.: John Wiley & Sons, 1967.

RISK ANALYSIS

This technique employs Monte Carlo simulation, and it enables management to identify, measure, and analyze uncertainties in investment problems.

D.B. Hertz, "Risk Analysis in Capital Investment" *Harvard Business Review,* January-February, 1964.

SAMPLING THEORY

A set of principles that permit an analyst to predict the characteristics of a large population on the basis of his findings about a small selection (the "sample") taken from that population.

L. Kish, *Survey Sampling.* New York, N.Y.: John Wiley & Sons, 1965.

SIMULATION (See "Operational Gaming")

SUBJECTIVE PROBABILITY (See "Probability")

TIME SERIES ANALYSIS

Techniques used to help understand the elements of change in a time series, and, as a result, to improve predictive techniques.

F.E. Croxton, D.J. Cowden, *Applied General Statistics.* Englewood Cliffs, N.J.: Prentice Hall, Inc., 1967.

Table B-1: Business Usage of Management Science Tools

	Techniques Most Used by Major Areas of Application															
	Finance		General Management		Logistics/ Distribution		Personnel		Production/ Manufacturing		Sales/ Marketing		Overall Gross Total[1]		Overall Net Total[1]	
Management Science Techniques	Number	Percent	Number	Percent	Number	Percent	Number	Percent	Number	Percent	Number	Percent	Number	Percent	Number	Percent
Accounting	94	58%	66	42%	26	23%	14	17%	31	25%	37	27%	268	35%	106	62%
Analysis of variance	35	22	30	19	12	11	14	17	33	27	50	36	174	22	85	49
Bayesian analysis	20	12	21	13	5	4	1	1	6	6	20	14	75	10	47	27
Break-even analysis	73	45	59	38	15	13	2	2	41	33	37	27	227	29	104	60
Calculus	24	15	28	18	21	19	8	10	31	25	23	17	135	17	61	36
Cluster analysis	8	5	13	8	3	3	10	12	9	7	34	25	77	10	53	31
Computer simulation[2]	103	64	86	55	71	63	19	23	76	61	56	41	411	53	148	86
Consumer behavior models	1	*	4	3	—	—	1	1	1	1	34	25	77	10	36	21
Cost accounting	56	35	42	27	21	19	8	10	38	30	20	14	185	24	82	48
Critical path/PERT	8	5	42	27	15	13	5	6	43	34	15	11	128	16	78	45
Decision tree analysis	35	22	58	37	14	12	6	7	23	18	29	21	165	21	82	48
Design of experiments	9	6	11	7	5	4	4	5	25	20	36	26	90	12	58	34
Difference equations	15	9	11	7	4	4	—	—	7	6	8	6	45	6	28	16
Discounted cash flow	135	84	82	52	13	12	2	2	27	22	25	18	284	37	145	84
Dynamic programming[3]	7	4	7	4	4	4	—	—	15	12	6	4	39	5	28	16
Exponential smoothing	25	15	27	17	23	20	4	5	37	30	60	43	176	23	107	62
Factor analysis	5	3	7	4	1	1	8	10	3	2	30	22	54	7	43	25
Game theory	5	3	18	11	3	3	—	—	4	3	12	9	42	5	29	17
Graph analysis	25	16	28	18	10	9	12	15	15	12	10	21	108	14	47	27
Heuristic methods	22	14	31	20	26	23	11	14	33	26	22	16	145	19	60	35
Information theory	9	6	9	6	4	4	4	5	3	2	6	4	35	4	16	9
Integer programming[3]	13	8	16	10	16	15	1	1	29	23	8	6	83	11	52	30
Linear programming[3]	40	25	44	28	62	55	4	5	75	60	33	24	258	33	121	70
Logical reasoning	60	37	74	47	53	47	40	49	54	43	56	41	337	44	83	48
Mapping	1	*	5	3	9	8	2	2	5	4	10	7	32	4	18	10
Mathematical programming[3]	26	16	29	18	32	28	4	5	36	29	24	17	151	20	61	36
Multivariate analysis	23	14	29	18	6	5	8	10	16	13	48	35	130	17	68	40
Nonlinear programming[3]	8	5	5	3	9	8	1	1	12	10	9	6	44	6	28	16
Probability theory	61	38	55	35	33	29	9	11	39	31	49	36	246	32	105	61
Probability geometry	4	2	2	2	2	2	1	1	3	2	3	2	15	2	7	4

Table B-1: Business Usage of Management Science Tools (continued)

Techniques Most Used by Major Areas of Application

Management Science Techniques	Finance		General Management		Logistics/ Distribution		Personnel		Production/ Manufacturing		Sales/ Marketing		Overall Gross Total[1]		Overall Net Total[1]	
	Number	Percent	Number	Percent	Number	Percent	Number	Percent	Number	Percent	Number	Percent	Number	Percent	Number	Percent
Queueing theory	5	3	9	6	25	22	1	1	32	26	6	4	78	10	55	32
Regression analysis	76	47	79	50	35	31	34	42	49	39	78	56	351	45	141	82
Risk analysis	84	52	56	35	10	9	2	2	23	18	41	30	216	28	111	64
Sampling theory	23	14	22	14	16	14	12	15	36	29	45	33	154	20	76	44
Sensitivity analysis	85	53	70	44	33	29	8	10	47	38	43	31	286	37	112	65
Simulation[2]	75	47	71	45	54	48	16	20	58	46	44	32	318	41	119	69
Statistical inference	24	15	33	21	18	16	12	15	25	20	38	28	150	19	67	39
Stochastic processes	10	6	15	9	11	10	4	5	16	13	11	8	67	9	37	22
Subjective probabilities	35	22	34	22	6	5	6	7	11	9	27	20	119	15	59	34
Time series analysis	51	32	47	30	19	17	11	14	34	27	68	49	230	30	109	63
Trade-off models	26	16	26	16	14	12	6	7	14	11	15	11	101	13	42	24
Base:	161	100%	158	100%	113	100%	81	100%	125	100%	138	100%	776	100%	172	100%
Net Simulation[2]	110	68	102	65	80	71	25	31	84	67	67	49	468	60	154	90
Net Programming[3]	62	38	54	34	72	64	6	7	90	72	45	33	329	42	138	80

Note: Counts are frequencies of mention by respondents; percentages are based on number of respondents indicating any usage in major application area, except Overall Gross Total column where base is total of all application area bases.

Shaded data indicate tool is among ten most frequently mentioned in one or more areas of application.

* Less than 1 percent.

– No mentions.

[1] Gross Total is: Sum of (number of respondents mentioning tool) (number of application areas mentioned); Net Total is: Sum of all respondents mentioning tool one or more times.

[2] Usage of these individual tools is combined in Net Simulation as the sum of all respondents mentioning one or more of these individual tools.

[3] Same as footnote 2 for Net Programming.

Table B-2: MS/OR Tools or Techniques Found Most Useful by Major Application Area and Overall

Major Areas of Application in Which Tools Are Found Most Useful

Management Science Techniques Found Most Useful:	Finance Number	Percent	General Management Number	Percent	Logistics/ Distribution Number	Percent	Personnel Number	Percent	Production/ Manufacturing Number	Percent	Sales/ Marketing Number	Percent	Overall Gross Total[1] Number	Percent	Overall Net Total[1] Number	Percent
Accounting	12	7%	11	7%	2	2%	1	1%	2	2%	1	1%	29	4%	18	18%
Analysis of variance	1	*	–	–	–	–	2	2	3	2	4	3	10	1	9	9
Bayesian analysis	–	–	–	–	1	1	–	–	–	–	1	1	2	*	2	2
Break-even analysis	5	3	5	3	–	–	–	–	–	–	4	3	14	2	10	10
Calculus	–	–	–	–	–	–	1	1	2	2	1	1	4	*	4	4
Cluster analysis	–	–	–	–	–	–	1	1	–	–	2	1	3	*	3	3
Computer simulation[2]	29	18	16	10	21	19	4	5	19	15	9	6	98	13	50	50
Consumer behavior	–	–	–	–	–	–	–	–	–	–	3	2	3	*	3	3
Cost accounting	6	4	–	–	–	–	–	–	6	5	1	1	13	2	10	10
Critical path/PERT	–	–	2	1	1	1	–	–	2	2	–	–	5	1	5	5
Decision tree analysis	1	*	7	4	–	–	2	2	2	2	5	4	17	2	16	16
Design of experiments	–	–	–	–	–	–	–	–	2	2	5	4	7	1	6	6
Difference equations	–	–	–	–	1	1	–	–	1	1	–	–	2	*	2	2
Discounted cash flow	34	21	11	7	–	–	–	–	2	2	3	2	50	6	40	40
Dynamic programming[3]	–	–	1	*	–	–	–	–	3	2	–	–	4	*	4	4
Exponential smoothing	1	*	1	*	2	2	–	–	2	2	5	4	11	1	11	11
Factor analysis	–	–	1	*	–	–	1	1	–	–	1	1	3	*	2	2
Game theory	–	–	2	1	–	–	–	–	–	–	1	1	3	*	3	3
Graph analysis	2	1	2	1	1	1	–	–	1	1	3	2	9	1	5	5
Heuristic methods	3	2	5	3	4	4	3	4	4	3	4	3	23	3	16	16
Information theory	–	–	–	–	1	1	–	–	–	–	–	–	1	*	1	1
Integer programming[3]	–	–	–	–	2	2	–	–	2	2	–	–	4	*	4	4
Linear programming[3]	1	*	7	4	19	17	–	–	25	20	7	5	59	8	34	34
Logical reasoning[3]	11	7	27	17	8	7	9	11	10	8	14	10	79	10	32	32
Mapping	–	–	–	–	2	2	–	–	–	–	–	–	2	*	2	2
Mathematical programming[3]	–	–	1	*	5	4	–	–	7	6	2	1	15	2	11	11
Multivariate analysis	3	2	5	3	1	1	2	2	1	1	5	4	17	2	10	10
Nonlinear programming[3]	–	–	–	–	–	–	–	–	1	1	2	1	3	*	3	3
Probability theory	3	2	3	2	2	2	–	–	1	1	5	4	14	2	13	13
Probability geometry	–	–	–	–	–	–	–	–	1	1	–	–	1	*	1	1

Table B-2: MS/OR Tools or Techniques Found Most Useful by Major Application Area and Overall (continued)

Major Areas of Application in Which Tools Are Found Most Useful

Management Science Techniques Found Most Useful:	Finance		General Management		Logistics/ Distribution		Personnel		Production/ Manufacturing		Sales/ Marketing		Overall Gross Total[1]		Overall Net Total[1]	
	Number	Percent	Number	Percent	Number	Percent	Number	Percent	Number	Percent	Number	Percent	Number	Percent	Number	Percent
Queueing theory	–	–	–	–	2	2	–	–	2	2	1	1	5	1	4	4
Regression analysis	7	4	12	8	1	1	6	7	5	4	14	10	45	6	34	34
Risk analysis	11	7	5	3	1	1	–	–	1	1	2	1	20	3	16	16
Sampling theory	1	*	1	*	–	–	2	2	5	4	5	4	14	2	13	13
Sensitivity analysis	8	5	9	6	2	2	–	–	2	2	3	2	24	3	20	20
Simulation[2]	9	6	8	5	3	3	1	1	9	7	3	2	33	4	23	23
Statistical inference	–	–	–	–	–	–	–	–	–	–	2	1	4	*	3	3
Stochastic processes	–	–	–	–	1	1	–	–	1	1	–	–	2	*	2	2
Subjective probabilities	–	–	1	*	–	–	–	–	–	–	1	1	2	*	2	2
Time series analysis	3	2	3	2	1	1	–	–	2	2	11	8	20	3	16	16
Trade-off models	2	1	2	1	1	1	–	–	–	–	3	2	8	1	6	6
Base:	161	100%	158	100%	113	100%	81	100%	125	100%	138	100%	776	100%	99	100%
Net Simulation[2]	33	20	27	17	22	20	6	6	24	19	11	8	111	14	60	60
Net Programming[3]	1	*	9	6	25	22	–	–	35	28	9	6	79	10	46	46

Note: Counts are frequencies of mention as "most useful" by respondents; percentages are based on number of respondents indicating any usage in major application areas, except Overall Gross Total column where base is total of all application area bases.

Shaded data indicate tool is among ten most frequently mentioned in one or more areas of application.

*Less than 1 percent.

–No mentions.

[1]Gross Total is: Sum of (number of respondents mentioning tool) (number of application areas mentioned); Net Total is: Sum of all respondents mentioning tool one or more times.

[2]Usage of these individual tools is combined in Net Simulation as the sum of all respondents mentioning one or more of these individual tools.

[3]Same as footnote 2 for Net Programming.

Appendix C
Management Science in Five Major Companies

MANAGEMENT SCIENCE PRACTICE in business is so varied that it is unlikely any one description could portray the full range of situations and activities confronting the typical unit. The following group of examples of units operating in specific contexts may help to suggest the variety of forms and labels under which MS activities are performed in business. Most of the cases presented here focus on the location of management science units within their company's organization and on their major activities. One – the Du Pont case – describes an exceptional instance of differentiated functions within the MS unit discussed.

We are especially grateful to the companies from whom these cases were drawn for their cooperation.

A Fully Articulated MS Organization (Standard Oil Company of California)

Standard Oil Company of California derives virtually all of its multibillion dollar annual revenues from one aspect or another of oil and its by-products – either exploration, production, transportation, refining or marketing. The giant, vertically integrated, multinational company's divisions, subsidiaries and affiliates operate around the world and are directed from its headquarters in San Francisco.

Management Science at Standard Oil

As with most other oil companies, large and not so large, Standard of California introduced MS/OR into its staff resources through the application of linear programming to the control and direction of

petroleum refining operations in the early 1950's. The company's Analytical Division – as the MS activity is labeled – was established at that time.

Subsequently, similar units were established throughout the major divisions and functional groupings of the company. While reporting directly to executives – usually financial – of the groups in which they work, these units remain under the technical oversight of the corporate analytical division head.

The corporate unit reports to the corporate comptroller who, in turn, reports to the Vice President-Finance (a company director). The latter is responsible to the three-person office of the chief executive. As is also the case with most of the other analytical division staffs (away from corporate headquarters), the corporate unit thus reports to what is approvingly described as a staff function with no direct profit-making responsibility and, hence, "a neutral, objective function, with no parochial axes to grind." The analytical division's reputation for impartiality in examining questions often fraught with internal political implications is felt to be derived, at least partially, from its neutral position. This image is stressed as an attribute that is jealously guarded by all the analytical units.

Corporate Vice Presidents Pose Projects

Much of the work of the corporate analytical division is brought by corporate officers. A major part of the division's MS effort comes from its responsibility for evaluation of the "benefits" section for virtually all capital appropriations requests over $10 million. (Requests for funds for exploration efforts are handled separately, within the exploration function, because of the extreme sensitivity of such information in the highly competitive search for new oil resources.)

The corporate analytical division's role is, however, far from passive. Its vantage point enables it to spot corporate problems in their earliest manifestations. The unit head reports that he can almost always find the sources to explore newly arising signs of trouble, at least to the point of being able to prepare an effectively documented proposal to initiate a broader investigation of the situation. Most of the other analytical units, being similarly located, react in a like fashion to "targets of opportunity."

Analytical Division: A Training Ground

While it is not uncommon to find many company hierarchies dotted with former MS/OR personnel who have moved up and out into higher staff or line positions, SoCal has institutionalized such movement into a staffing policy for the analytical division. An elaborate and formal screen-and-search procedure – operated with SoCal's office of executive development – brings technically competent, bright new people who are sophisticated in business knowledge from all over the company into the corporate analytical division for a two- or three-year stint. This process serves as a training exercise for the recruits and as a constant renewal of fresh viewpoints to the function's problem-solving work.

The staffing policy requires careful attention, the corporate division's head reports, especially in regard to balancing the flow between those individuals selected by the process who prefer not to "get stuck in a think tank" and those who, having experienced the analytical environment, prefer not to move back outside it.

In addition to the head of the division, a staff of 20 professionals comprises the corporate analytical division. Five of them are geologists, geophysicists and petroleum engineers from the company's exploration and production areas. Another five, described as "business types," have backgrounds in accounting, finance or marketing, with either MBA degrees or graduate degrees in economics. Nine more are from research, manufacturing or engineering groups; most of them are chemical engineers, and are identified as "process-types." The twentieth position in the group is filled by a recent MBA graduate, passing through as part of his entry training with the company. The MBA trainee is the only staff member accepted under 30 years of age (and for less than a two- to three-year assignment), since a prime prerequisite for the other candidates is significant experience and exposure within the company. Many of the staff have doctorates in their specialty; all have solid grounding in mathematics, though not necessarily in the specific techniques traditionally ascribed to MS/OR.

A by-product benefit of the rotation policy is its contribution to the division's work; it has been cited as making the work both more effective and more gratifying. The upper levels of SoCal's management are dotted with analytical division "alumni," who not only provide the usual connective apparatus of the "old-school-tie" network but bring serious and significant problems to their former shop's attention. Three of the 16 corporate vice presidents are former analytical division members; two of the three executives comprising the office of the chief executive are also; and the manager of corporate planning and three of his staff members came from the analytical division as well.

A potential disadvantage of the rotation policy lies in the constant departure of experienced analytical division professionals. The practice of carefully documenting the progress, findings and recommendations of all projects is, in part, a means of minimizing the turnover effects, although, of course, maintaining permanent records meets other objectives, also.

The present head of the division tries to assign people with a substantive background in one area of the company's business to project task forces working in totally different areas. Again, this affords the individuals enhanced opportunities to broaden their experience, while ensuring that the analysts examining a problem will be taking a fresh look.

The Analytical Division's Design of Tools

Over the years, the analytical division has developed a large number of computerized mathematical models as tools for its work. Originally, the division designed the basic layouts itself, with the computer staff providing only final programming and implementation. Since the mid-1960's, however, the computer services group has passed the analytical division's capabilities in this field. The division now turns over its design specifications to the computer staff for systems development, implementation, and maintenance.

Among the basic tools built by the analytical division is a calculating module called an "actuarial rate of return" (AROR) model. This module can be engaged through interactive terminals and performs rate-of-return calculations with a wide variety of user assumptions, including tax and cost-of-funds considerations. Outputs are provided in a range of formats, including returns to a variety of initial bases, pro forma profit-and-loss statements, cash-flow projections, payout-period projections, et cetera. Essentially a highly flexible, easily activated calculator, AROR is described as an extremely useful instant investment-project evaluator. Other analytical divisions, taking the basic AROR package, have successfully adapted it to their own specialized needs – when estimating rates-of-return on risky exploration proposals, to take one example.

Another major tool is a bidding model that supports SoCal's bonus-bidding strategies and tactics in seeking federal acreage allotments, primarily in the offshore areas as they open up. An ongoing study of historical patterns of recent bidding behavior is aimed at a better understanding of competitive strategies and their economic consequences, particularly in the light of the newly evidenced dynamism of oil and energy economics.

Combining a queueing theory model with a general purpose simulation system, the corporate analytical division has provided SoCal with the ability to study and alter the design of a major overseas bulk storage, transshipment, and refinery facility. This was done in order to minimize cost and maximize transshipment and production efficiencies. This facility design model led the division to develop a ship strategy model that helps resolve the build-buy-or-charter decisions SoCal constantly confronts in regard to its oil fleet.

Evolution of Refinery Technology

The early application of linear programming technology to aggregate refinery scheduling set up strong expectations throughout the oil industry – expectations of a quick progression to the day of "hands-off," completely automated refineries that would be run entirely by computers. While the conceptualizers were willing, the technology was weak and, today, relatively few refineries have approached such a state of automated control. Only the newest operate in anything like a state of "direct digital control."

In recent years refinery technology has advanced to a degree of flexibility and precision that encouraged SoCal – and most other oil companies – to renew efforts to build and operate direct digital-control models for hands-off refinery operations. At the same time, the advanced design capabilities provided by the newest refinery equipment have opened up fresh opportunities for developing production strategies as well as strategies for refinery design.

The analytical division has acquired a package for simulating refinery operations under linear programming. This simulator permits the division to carry out what is described as "very sophisticated" refinery operations simulations, as well as to model a wide variety of highly flexible equipment alternatives. By adding, deleting, combining and recombining units of refinery technology in building-block fashion, they are able to approach 100-percent optimality for specific refinery installation designs.

Energy Crisis Brings New Problems

Of course, the dramatic shift in oil economics and politics since 1973 has posed many new and challenging problems to Standard of California and its competitors. Not the least of these problems is one that provided a new impetus to improve controls over work-in-process inventories at Standard of California's refineries. Before crude oil prices multiplied from their traditional cost-of-recovery basis, refinery working capital costs were considered a relatively modest factor in refinery operations. For example, a $200 million refinery might carry a feed-stock inventory averaging $50 million or less before 1973; the jump in crude prices almost immediately raised feed-stock values to the level of the investment in the refinery itself. Thus, a newly sharpened imperative for inventory controls and models for projecting working-capital and cash-flow requirements was created. Most of the analytical division's work is performed through the medium of informal task forces, set up with leadership responsibility assigned to particular contact people in the substantive operating organization and one or more of the analytical division's personnel assigned to do the required analytical work.

Chevron Exhibit 1: Distribution of MS Units in Standard Oil Company of California, CHEVRON U.S.A., Inc.

President
Executive Vice President
*Vice-President Finance
Vice-President & General Counsel Legal
Vice-President Washington, D. C., Office
Vice-President Public Affairs
Vice-President Industrial Relations
Regional Vice-President General Representation
General Manager Environmental Affairs
General Manager Organization
Management Staff
Senior Vice-President Exploration, Land and Production
*Manager Planning and Analysis
Coordinator Exploration
Coordinator Production
Coordinator Production Operations and Projects
Regional Vice-Presidents (three)
Senior Vice-President Manufacturing, Supply and Marketing
*Vice-President Manufacturing
*Vice-President Supply
*Vice-President Marketing
*General Manager Planning and Analysis
Manager Product Engineering
Manager Petroleum Regulations

*Includes analytical unit.

Little Budgetary Restraint

The corporate analytical division reports that it is under no uncomfortable budgetary restraint, except in one area. The division head has been under some criticism for the unreliability of his estimates of computational costs. These, he notes, have recently been difficult to estimate because so much of the division's work has been done on a spot-demand basis, involving significant amounts of computer time on an unscheduled, unpredictable basis.

In addition to the corporate analytical division, located in the comptrollership function of the corporate finance staff, analytical units are located in the following major components of Standard Oil of California's organization:

Corporate Staff Components:
Supply and Distribution
Tax
Treasurer's Office
Foreign Operations Staff
Planning Staff

Operating Components:
Chevron Oil Europe, Inc.
Chevron Canada, Ltd.
Chevron Standard, Ltd.
Chevron International Oil Co., Inc.
Chevron Shipping Co.
Chevron Overseas Petroleum, Inc.
Chevron Chemical Co.
Chevron Land and Development Co.
Chevron Resources Division of Chevron Industries, Inc.
Chevron U.S.A.

A detailed line chart, accompanying, displays the distribution of analytical units in a major SO-CAL operating component.

A Major Management Science Resource in R and D at Westinghouse Electric Corporation

A major management science resource for Westinghouse Electric Corporation is located in its Research and Development Center, where it is known as the systems sciences unit (see Exhibit 2, page 73). It resides within the *applied* sciences research division of the R and D Center.

Exhibit 2: Schematic Relationship of Systems Sciences Unit to Westinghouse Hierarchy

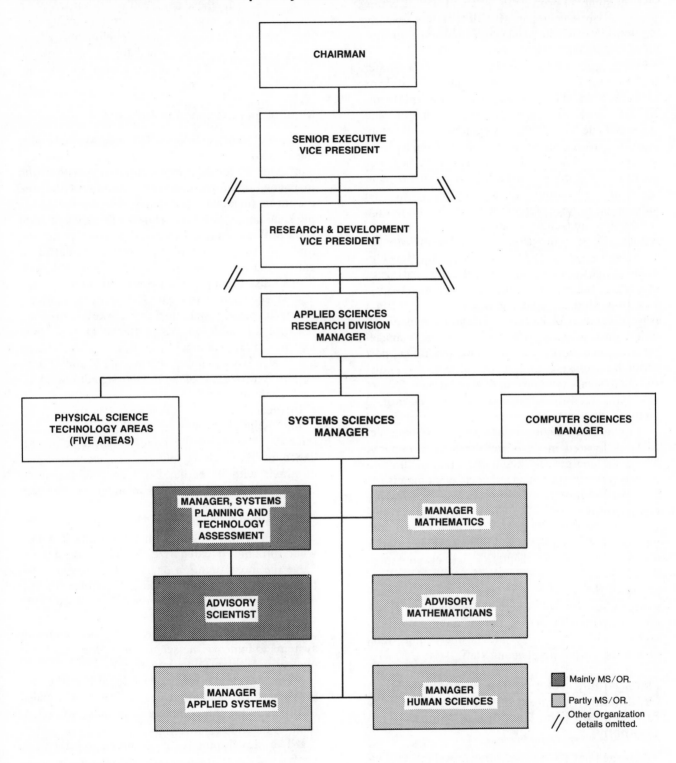

Established in the late 1950's, the total unit consists of some 40 professionals, about half of whom are primarily engaged in MS/OR activities. Nearly three-fourths of the management science professionals have earned doctoral degrees.

Apparently, its location in the R and D Center has not inhibited its access to significant problems elsewhere in the company. The unit performs MS/OR work for "any corporate-level unit and does outside consulting," according to its manager. Its project range parallels that of the average management science unit studied, with a major share of its emphasis turned toward general management applications. In addition, it carries on substantial project commitments in the marketing, production and finance areas, as well as more modest efforts in the personnel and logistics areas.

Individual projects have included the development of market forecasting models, the analysis of strategic plans, minimum-cost product-optimization studies, and the analysis of product price-escalation procedures. The other half of the unit's professionals, who also do some management science work, provides more general support through technical consulting in mathematics, statistics, physical systems analysis, human factors analysis, technological assessment, economic analysis, and so forth.

Another Westinghouse management science activity is located in its Power Systems Company. There an energy and economic analysis unit in power-systems marketing supports planning efforts for Westinghouse's major power-generating equipment divisions. The two units, in power systems and the R and D Center, have no formal connections with each other and pursue their activities for their respective clientele relatively independently. They do, however, join forces in the preparation of the yearly forecasts for power systems' planning overview. Additional management science practitioners are scattered among Westinghouse's company, group and business unit staffs and in the corporate planning staff.

Management Science in a Financial/MIS Organization Context and an R and D Environment (The Babcock & Wilcox Company)

Management science/operations research was introduced into The Babcock & Wilcox Company, a major steam-generating and nuclear-energy equipment maker, in the early 1960's. Its introduction originated, in a large degree, from the urging of a vice president of research and development whose prior experience in the armed forces had brought him into close contact with operations research activities.

Management Science at Babcock & Wilcox

The OR unit, employing 12 professionals plus the director, is part of the corporate headquarters staff and is located organizationally within the management-information-services function of the corporate financial organization (see Exhibit 3). Its physical home, however, is in the facilities of Babcock & Wilcox's research and development laboratories in Alliance, Ohio. The OR unit's neutral location may account for its uniformly balanced project list among the major applications areas; almost equal emphasis exists on general management, financial, production and marketing area applications. In addition to a scattering of projects in logistics and personnel, the Babcock & Wilcox group also works on engineering and R and D projects to improve the planning and scheduling of efforts in these areas.

In recent years, the OR group has found itself being assigned broad responsibilities more frequently for studying the issues of strategic significance to Babcock & Wilcox management. This contrasts with its earlier experience of providing one or more professionals as members of "project teams" or "task forces."

With a flow of some 50 to 80 projects a year, the operations research unit's director finds it somewhat difficult to categorize the projects that receive the most attention or make the greatest contribution. Among outstanding examples in the unit's history are these projects:

• The design of long-range production planning systems to improve the scheduling of long-leadtime nuclear energy system components;
• The developing of models to aid in the improvement of metallurgical and structural quality of products for the company's specialty steel production facilities;
• The development of planning models for analysis of operating and corporate components.
• The building of simulations of shop conditions

Exhibit 3: Management Science in a Financial/MIS Organization Context and an Operations Environment: The Babcock & Wilcox Company

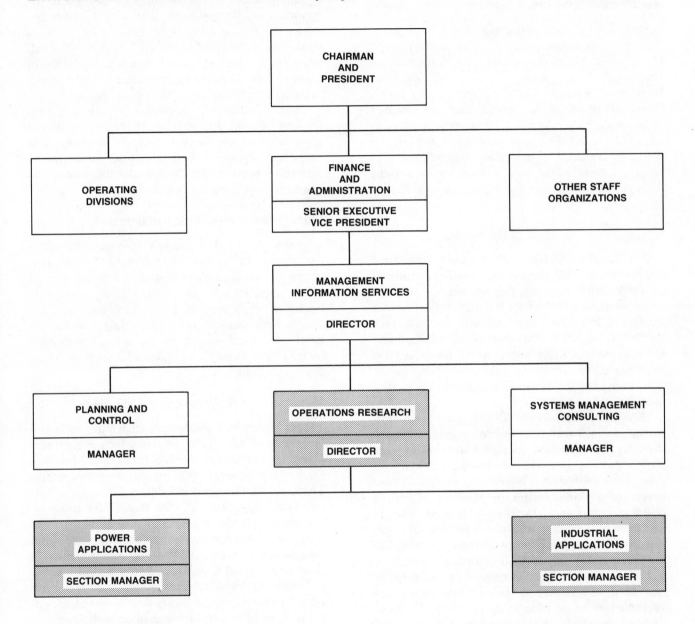

to test alternatives for improving shop throughput in production studies; and

• Economic forecasting using inflation indexes as guides to pricing and revenue projections.

Reflecting Babcock & Wilcox's two major industrial orientations, the MS/OR unit's analysts are organized into two subunits – one associated more closely with the power-generating group, the other associated with the industrial products group. Neither management science subunit is committed exclusively to the two major groups, thereby allowing sufficient flexibility for the best resource allocation.

A Differentiated Approach to Management Science Careers at E. I. du Pont de Nemours & Co., Inc.

The lack of any conscious division of labor among management scientists has been noted.[1] Usually, the MS professionals refer to themselves simply as "scientists," "analysts" or "researchers," without specifying the various levels or aspects of the work to which they are assigned or in which they specialize. While practitioners in the field realize that some colleagues tend to be better in certain MS specialties than others, it is relatively rare to find such differences in abilities or interests reflected in the organization of an MS unit.

Management Science at Du Pont

E. I. du Pont de Nemours' largest management science group – the Business Consulting Section of its Information Systems Department – has three principal career ladders for its staff, reflecting differing emphasis on phases of MS/OR work (see Exhibit 4, page 77). This centralized management science group carries out projects for many Du Pont businesses – especially those involving use of the company's centralized data-processing facilities.

This group's principal MS/OR branches – MS consulting, MS technical and MS administrative – stem from a common root of management specialists and analysts, plus two entry-level positions – business analyst and industrial engineer. These latter two positions reflect the general preferences revealed in this study for analysts trained either in quantitative business analysis or in industrial engineering. The basic elements of their position descriptions differ only in their analytical focus. The business analyst's function emphasizes performing mathematical analyses of business data to support overall plans of solution to client problems; these problems generally deal with production, financial or material resources. The description of the industrial engineer's parallel position discusses performing engineering analyses of business situations to support overall solution plans applied to client problems that generally deal with the impact upon Du Pont's human resources.

[1] See Stanley J. PoKempner, "Is There a Management Scientist in the House?" *The Conference Board RECORD,* May, 1974, pp. 11-15.

Management Sciences: Consulting

The position guides of the two top steps described as "Management Sciences, Consulting" stress the liaison aspects of management science work (see Exhibit 5, page 78). These are the MS practitioners whose special aptitudes include unusual ability to communicate with their managerial counterparts in exploring MS opportunities.

These "interface" specialists possess top professional qualifications that they exercise in the application of advanced technical knowledge and analytical abilities. Their decisions on technical matters represent the final authority within the business consulting section.

Management Sciences: Technical

These are the MS group's management scientists, who are responsible for methods research, development, implementation, and improvement of MS methodology for Du Pont. Usually specialists in one or more specific areas of management science's mathematical repertoire, they concentrate on the technical aspects of the group's activities, leaving most client or administrative matters to the other two branches.

Management Sciences: Administrative

This branch has two steps, each utilizing a different set of MS skills, among which are project planning and direction, MS personnel development, and general MS project administration. These practitioners review detailed cost-and-effort estimates, negotiate MS "contracts" for projects, and carry out the managerial and administrative tasks to keep the projects on schedule and within budget. In addition, they guide subordinates in their professional training and growth. Although a high level of technical competence is shared with other branches, the emphasis here is on the administration of MS work rather than on technique.

Other MS Work at Du Pont

The position guides described here pertain only to Du Pont's most articulated MS function: the Business Consulting Section of the corporate Information Systems Department. Other Du Pont MS activities are found in various components where the volume of specialized analysis work requires them – e.g., in marketing research, business planning, production methods units.

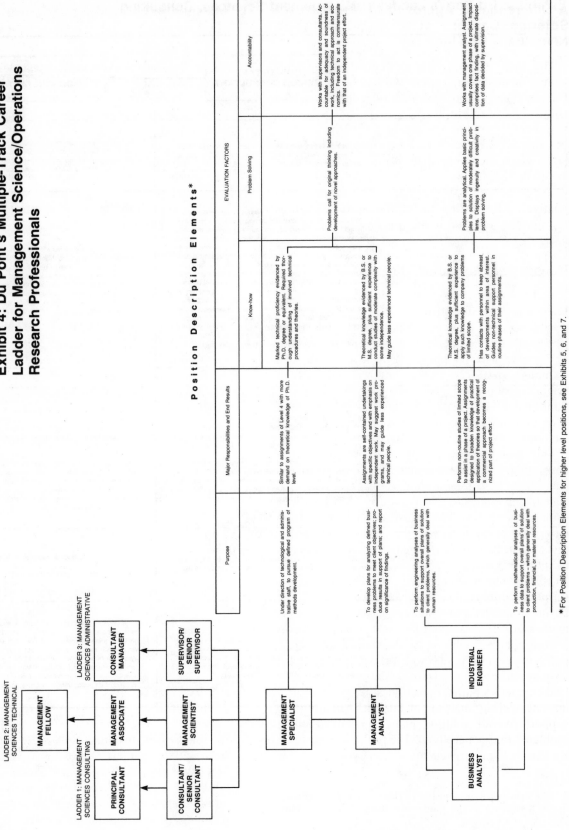

Exhibit 4: Du Pont's Multiple-Track Career Ladder for Management Science/Operations Research Professionals

Position Description Elements*

Purpose	Major Responsibilities and End Results	Know-how	Problem Solving	Accountability
			EVALUATION FACTORS	
Under direction of technological and administrative staff, to pursue defined program of methods development.	Similar to assignments of Level 4 with more demand on theoretical knowledge of Ph.D. level.	Marked technical proficiency evidenced by Ph.D. degree or equivalent. Required thorough understanding of involved technical procedures and theories.	Problems call for original thinking including development of novel approaches.	Works with supervisors and consultants. Accountable for adequacy and soundness of work, including technical approach and economics. Freedom to act is commensurate with that of an independent project effort.
To develop plans for analyzing defined business problems to meet client objectives; produce results in support of plans; and report on significance of findings.	Assignments are self-contained undertakings with specific objectives and with emphasis on independent work. May suggest work programs, and may guide less experienced technical people.	Theoretical knowledge evidenced by B.S. or M.S. degree, plus sufficient experience to conduct studies of moderate complexity with some independence. May guide less experienced technical people.		
To perform engineering analyses of business situations to support overall plans of solution to client problems, which generally deal with human resources.	Performs non-routine studies of limited scope to assist in a phase of a project. Assignments designed to broaden knowledge of practical application of theories so that development of a commercial approach becomes a recognized part of project effort.	Theoretical knowledge evidenced by B.S. or M.S. degree, plus sufficient experience to apply such knowledge to company problems of limited scope.	Problems are analytical. Applies basic principles to solution of moderately difficult problems. Displays ingenuity and creativity in problem solving.	Works with management analyst. Assignment usually covers one phase of a project. Impact comprises fact finding, with ultimate disposition of data decided by supervision.
To perform mathematical analyses of business data to support overall plans of solution to client problems – which generally deal with production, financial, or material resources.		Has contacts with personnel to keep abreast of developments within area of interest. Guides non-technical support personnel in routine phases of their assignments.		

Position Description Elements*

* For Position Description Elements for higher level positions, see Exhibits 5, 6, and 7.

LADDER 2: MANAGEMENT SCIENCES TECHNICAL

LADDER 3: MANAGEMENT SCIENCES ADMINISTRATIVE

LADDER 1: MANAGEMENT SCIENCES CONSULTING

MANAGEMENT FELLOW

CONSULTANT MANAGER

MANAGEMENT ASSOCIATE

SUPERVISOR/ SENIOR SUPERVISOR

PRINCIPAL CONSULTANT

MANAGEMENT SCIENTIST

CONSULTANT/ SENIOR CONSULTANT

MANAGEMENT SPECIALIST

MANAGEMENT ANALYST

INDUSTRIAL ENGINEER

BUSINESS ANALYST

Exhibit 5: Du Pont's Ladder 1: Management Sciences, Consulting

TITLE	CONSULTANT/ SENIOR CONSULTANT →	PRINCIPAL CONSULTANT
Purpose	To provide liaison with client managers, to increase utilization with Du Pont of management science methodologies, and to recommend solutions to client problems.	To provide liaison with client executives to increase utilization within Du Pont of major new management science methodologies; to maintain an independent client contact base; and generally to deal with unstructured problems.
Major Responsibilities and End Results	Provides consulting services to various company operations to assist in solving complex company problems requiring broad technical competence and mature judgment; develops programs for, conducts, and coordinates major studies, utilizing the services of Du Pont groups, and outside consultants when they are required to assist company organization in maintaining technology ahead of competitors; coordinates activities of diverse groups on broad programs to give qualified overall direction on major problems; maintains effective communications in the development and application of technology in the specific field (Contacts may include all levels of management, vendors, other companies, state or local agencies, technical societies and may involve negotiations with these agencies in the company interest); provides assistance in training, safety leadership and other group functions and guides less experienced personnel.	Provides advice and consultation to various company operations to assist in solving highly technical problems; represents the Department and Du Pont Company with technical societies, educational institutions and government agencies to bring authoritative knowledge to these organizations; adds to company technology through documenting formal studies and thereby enhancing the company's economic and competitive position.
EVALUATION FACTORS		
Know-how	In a given field of technology: (1) Advanced technical knowledge of problems across several company departments as evidenced by Bachelor's degree or the equivalent, plus at least 10-17 years applicable experience; (2) Demonstrated ability to develop solutions to complex problems, documented by studies and presentations to professional societies. Results of consulting services as supported by company client acceptance and recognition is a controlling factor in reaching this level of responsibility.	(1) Comprehensive and authoritative knowledge of a particular field, represented by outstanding achievements. Such depth, breadth of knowledge and achievement would have been gained through broad contact with problems through a period of at least 11 to 18 years. (2) Ability to develop solutions to complex problems, with very little technical guidance, demonstrated by studies and documented savings of considerable importance to the company's economic and competitive position. (3) Recognition as a leading authority in his field, throughout the company and nationally, is a controlling factor for this level of technical responsibility.
Problem Solving	Creative and original thinking required for solving unique problems. Must evaluate alternate courses of action and make recommendations supported by authoritative reasoning.	Requires highly developed analytical ability and high technical competence. Assignments may have little precedent, requiring originality and creative thinking.
Accountability	Administrative guidance from Consultant Manager. Decisions represent the final authority on technical matters within the field. Because of professional status within the company recommendations have an important effect. Accountability is shared with client departments and magnitude of end results would be in range of $100M to $1MM annually.	Administrative guidance from section manager, Recommendations carry considerable influence, and conclusions generally relate to problems of significant economic importance which may have wide impact through the company. Magnitude of end results influenced by this position would generally range from $100M to $1MM. $100M – $1MM represent range in which average of recommended changes would cost for replacements, changes, modifications, etc.

Exhibit 6: Du Pont's Ladder 2: Management Sciences, Technical

TITLE	MANAGEMENT SCIENTIST	→ MANAGEMENT ASSOCIATE	→ MANAGEMENT FELLOW
Purpose	To pursue independent program of methods development for clearly defined objectives.	To formulate plans for developing and/or implementing new methodologies of value to Du Pont; to pursue an independent program of methods development; and to support consultancy to client management in unstructured problems.	To establish technology development programs within areas of departmental interest determining direction section will follow in future years.
Major Responsibilities and End Results	Formulates attack on highly complex problems. Recommends programs and participates in establishing priorities. Assembles all available information and specifies appropriate facilities and assistance. Directs course of project subject to periodic review and approval of interim recommendations.	Conceives and originates project ideas within the framework of departmental goals. Self-generated programs require taking considerable initiative in finding new approaches to objectives, evaluating alternates and taking risks.	Considerable reliance placed on incumbent's selection of studies that will provide maximum utilization of his knowledge with respect to ultimate company benefit. Assignments also generated by problems confronting other personnel and requiring an unusually high level of knowledge in incumbent's field. Advises management on technical feasibility of important proposals.
EVALUATION FACTORS			
Know-how	Demonstrated competence in advanced technology of his discipline. Also competent in techniques of organizing and guiding a research project. Must have made significant contributions in the technical field and demonstrated a strong aptitude for problem solving and experimentation. Must keep current with new technology. May supervise one or more technical people.	Thorough appreciation and understanding of the development approach to problems with broad technical knowledge and highly developed expertise in a given field. Recognized authority in his discipline. Must keep current with new technology. May direct activities of one or more technical people. Able to effectively communicate technical counsel to others.	Incumbent's unique mastery and know-how of a particular field is such as to identify the individual as singularly outstanding in the company. In fields not restricted to company interests this depth of knowledge would command the same level of recognition across the profession. Provides technical leadership to others as required. Wide recognition in field dictates a broad range of contacts both within and outside the company.
Problem Solving	Makes comprehensive analysis of all aspects of complex problems including intangible considerations as well as physical factors.	Thinking guided and circumscribed by the general technical principles and practical considerations such as cost, utility and related factors. Development of novel or non-recurring pathfinding approaches is required with few guide posts.	Involvement with problems whose technical complexity requires approaches consistent with fundamental technology development efforts.
Accountability	Works with Consultant Manager. Accountable for conducting competent and thoroughly professional investigations in the field of his discipline. Responsible for reviewing and explaining project results to all levels of management, and for evaluating results and making sound recommendations on furtherance of the business.	Works with Section Manager. Through creative ability and development activity, can have a marked effect in uncovering new opportunities for the department. Freedom to act is such that incumbent has a controlling impact on the end results of his activities.	Accountable for selection of programs, recommendations for continuing or discontinuing projects and for attaining objectives. Conclusions reached generally relate to problems of significant economic importance and may have wide impact within the company.

Exhibit 7: Du Pont's Ladder 3: Management Sciences, Administrative

TITLE	SUPERVISOR/ SENIOR SUPERVISOR	→	CONSULTANT MANAGER
Purpose	To supervise application of a specific consulting service, including project planning and results, personnel development and general administration.		To meet established section objectives, allocate manpower and control funding where necessary to meet plan, and coordinate internal (overhead) activities between supervisory groupings.
Major Responsibilities and End Results	Determines type and number of people required for work programs; maintains close check over costs and relations with clients to meet the consulting needs of industrial and auxiliary departments; plans and schedules work programs to provide proper guidance and direction to group effort; establishes and maintains productive and harmonious relations with other groups to analyze company's needs and gain acceptance of the group's services; guides subordinate positions in developing evaluations, selection of best of several alternate methods, and presentation of recommendations so that individual members of the group receive proper training and development and are recognized as professionally competent.		Negotiates contracts for new work, oversees group progress and expenditures, conducts performance reviews, handles personnel problems, maintains contact with activities throughout the company in assigned area of systems work, determines personnel requirements.
EVALUATION FACTORS			
Know-how	Bachelor's degree or equivalent, plus minimum applicable experience of from 9-16 years. (Experience must provide suitable background for assuming supervisory responsibility.) Thorough understanding of technology of the particular field. Ability to develop less experienced personnel and to promote consulting services with client departments.		Bachelor's degree or equivalent. Human relations and coordination skills are critical. Broad knowledge of company accounting and operations, and wide acquaintance with key personnel in operating and staff departments. At least 15 years of experience in both technical and administrative capacities.
Problem Solving	High analytical ability to guide and direct group programs in light of company needs. Must decide on new study proposals and review and pass on major recommendations from the group.		Problem areas are ill-defined, involve complex business situations, and require imaginative solutions.
Accountability	General guidance and review by Consultant Manager. Accountable for development of new programs and resulting recommendations. Recommendations made to clients often involve advanced technological thinking which cannot be completely checked by supervision. Final accountability is shared with clients who have the authority to implement study recommendations. Magnitude of end results affected by the position would range from $100M to $1MM annually.		Guided by management. Group budget is up to $1MM a year.

Exhibit 8: Technical Support Orientation of Management Science/Operations Research Units: Owens-Illinois, Inc.

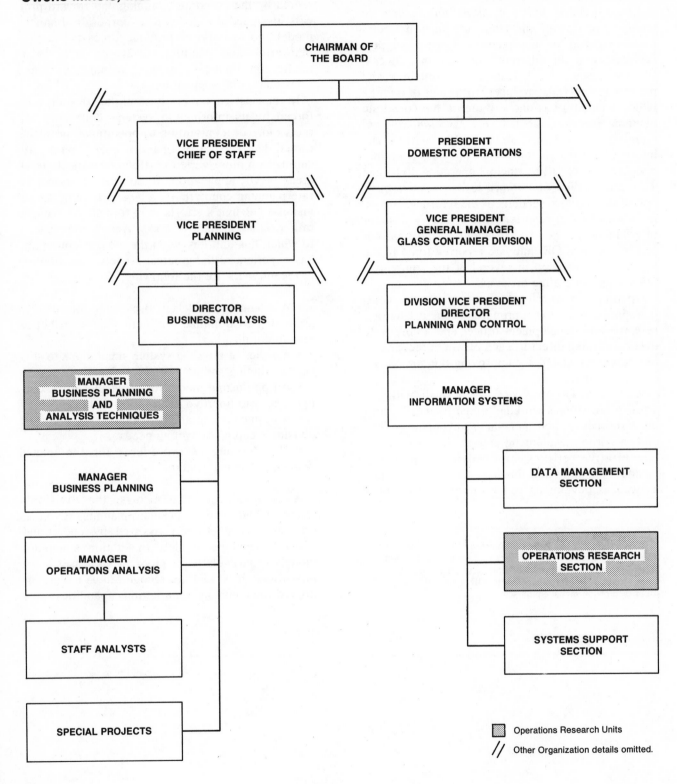

Independent Operations Research Units at Owens-Illinois, Inc.

Two unrelated units, each within a separate technical-service of the company, furnish operations research or management science support services in quite different areas of the Owens-Illinois organization.[2] This major container and packaging materials producer (with sales of over $2 billion annually) has one key unit in the corporate planning function, labeled *business planning and analysis techniques,* and another within the information-systems function of the glass container division, one of O-I's principal operating divisions. This unit, called *operations research section,* is one of three major sections of the information systems activity that reports to the division's director of planning and control. In addition, informal nuclei of potential OR units are reported to be in the process of formation in several of the company's other major operating divisions.

Operations research activities began at this company in the late 1960's, primarily at the urging of a research and development officer and a corporate data-processing director, each of whom recognized the potentials of OR for improving the company's decision making.

Each of the O-I units is relatively small, with just a few professionals working primarily at OR, sharing resources in their immediate surroundings. The unit in corporate planning engages in a variety of consultative efforts and advises on many business-planning and financial-analysis problems, as well as developing general-purpose mathemat-

ical tools and techniques for corporate planning needs. More concentrated attention has been directed by the corporate planning unit toward projects designed to develop a corporate financial model and to improve product forecasts in sales-marketing and production. Its projects focus mainly on financial, general management, and sales-marketing applications.

In the glass container division, the OR unit, reinforced by its information systems colleagues, directs more of its attention to operational problems rather than general or financial ones, thereby resulting in a more varied portfolio of projects in all areas of OR application. In contrast to its corporate planning counterpart, a larger share of the divisional OR unit's efforts is in formalized projects rather than consultative tasks. Among the projects to which this unit has given the most attention and has experienced the greatest sense of contribution in recent years are the following:

- A planning model incorporating linear programming to optimize production-and-distribution resource utilization.
- A series of physical system simulations to support marketing and new product planning.
- An optimizing model for box-pallet-truck configurations to improve distribution practices.
- A design for a strategic planning system for the division's capital budgeting needs.
- The devising of procedures for the annual financial-planning system.

As a result of such efforts, the division's strategic and tactical business-planning activities are said to be strongly assisted by operations-research developed models. In addition, simulation models – particularly of physical processes – are now widely used and are recognized as having improved the company's marketing capabilities.

---

[2] "Operations research" is the preferred terminology in O-I where the "management sciences" are associated with a broader conglomeration of the behavioral sciences, social and other sciences, and the business arts. OR is viewed as a specific subbranch of the management sciences.

Appendix D
Survey Design and Composition of Respondents

THE SURVEY RESEARCH underlying most of this report was conducted in two principal stages: The first, a screening phase, collected data on the incidence of management science/operations research units in companies. The second, utilizing the incidence data, collected responses on a wide range of activities and practices of MS/OR units through three sequential questionnaires to the heads of these units.

The screening questionnaire was sent to slightly more than 1,250 companies' senior personnel executives. These were drawn at random from the 1,000 largest industrial companies and representative samples of smaller industrial companies, insurance companies, banks and other financial institutions, retail and wholesale trade firms, public utilities, construction firms, transportation companies, and other service companies. Professional service firms (public accountants, management consultants, and so forth) who might offer MS consulting services were omitted. Each of the firms was identified by its size (measured by the number of employees), its principal business (by its primary two-digit Standard Industrial Classification code), and its geographic location (zip codes).

The sample was designed to draw higher proportions of both larger and industrial firms than of smaller or service companies based on a priori evidence of the firms' likelihood of having MS/OR units. The final screening sample, therefore, was selected by applying disproportionate weights to the several strata, first by size and then by type of business.

Response Rates

The sample of screening respondents resulted in a typical return of questionnaires of 484 usable responses – just under 40 percent. The overall response rate, of course, masks the differential response rates among the several classes of businesses sampled. Again, in line with experience, larger firms responded at higher rates than smaller ones, industrial firms replied at average rates, while transportation/utility companies responded at higher than average rates, and other service-type businesses replied at lower rates (see Table D-2, page 85).

The respondents to the screening survey provided two basic forms of information: First, they indicated whether or not their firms had any management science/operations research units; and, second, if they had, they identified these units by providing the names and addresses of the unit managers. These data provide the basis for estimates of the incidence of MS/OR units in business firms and the frame for the sample of MS/OR managers who contributed the substantive data for this report.

The disproportionalities induced by both the sample design and the response rates combine to make questionable the value of projecting the responses to an estimate of the total population of business firms. However, a very crude estimate of the population values of the incidence data (using the "number-of-employees" size classes of the Bureau of the Census) yields a ball park "guess"

Table D-1: Company Characteristics Employed in Sample Selection and Respondent Identification

A. Size Characteristic, Number of Employees

Initial Cells Employee Classes	Final Reporting Classes
100,000 and over 50,000 - 99,999	Large
25,000 - 49,999 10,000 - 24,999	Medium
5,000 - 9,999 2,500 - 4,999 1,000 - 2,499 500 - 999	Small
250 - 499 0 - 249	(Dropped)

B. Type of Business, Standard Industrial Classification Codes

Two-Digit SIC Codes			
01 - 09	Agriculture		
10 - 14	Mining, Extraction	Nonmanufacturing	Industrial
15 - 17	Construction		
20 - 39	Manufacturing	Manufacturing	
40 - 49	Transportation/ Utilities	Transportation/Utilities	
50 - 59	Trade		Services
70 - 89	Services	Trade/Services	
60 - 67	Financial	Financial	

that about a fifth of all U.S. firms with over 500 employees have units that carry on activities covered in the definition of management science/operations research used in this report:[1]

[1] The estimate of a "fifth" here is corrected for the 41 managers of units identified as management science units who, in the substantive survey of MS practices, disavowed the identification (see page 87). Prior to correction the estimate was just under 25 percent. Both estimates are for the incidence of *management science units* only and do not include, for example, firms who have individual MS practitioners providing essentially similar services. The screening survey also provided evidence that a number of the personnel executives responding failed to identify *known* MS/OR units in their firms. Since it was not possible to verify every instance of mis-identification in this direction, no compensating adjustment for under-reporting of MS/OR units is available.

" 'Management Science' refers to the systematic study of managerial systems, relying heavily on quantitative and mathematical analytical techniques applied within the perspectives of the 'soft' (social) and 'hard' (physical) science disciplines. For the purposes of this phase of the study, a management science component is *any* staff unit established primarily to apply the tools and techniques of quantitative or mathematical analysis to the study of and improvement of managerial systems."

(In addition, explicit recognition was expressed of the likelihood of units doing MS/OR work having widely varying labels. The inquiry concentrated on the scope of MS/OR work and the context in which it is performed.)

The Substantive Sample

Among the companies reporting that they have MS/OR units, an average of 2.5 units per company was identified. The great majority of these reported only one such unit; among those reporting multiple units, the most reported by a firm was over 20 units.

From the over 500 units identified – augmented by a few additional units identified independently – a set of MS/OR managers was selected for the substantive three-part survey.

A single comprehensive questionnaire was considered by a combined group of management science practitioners, professional society officers, and academicians, to be both too lengthy and, in some critical respects, incomplete. Consequently, a number of questioning areas were deleted and, at the recommendation of several of the reviewers, the single questionnaire was redesigned into three survey instruments, each significantly briefer than the original.

It is moot as to whether or not the sequential questioning significantly altered the achieved response rate from what might have been expected from the single comprehensive instrument. Not all the respondents completed all three questionnaires (see Table D-5, page 87). In addition, of course, response rates varied by individual questions.

The basic structure of the substantive survey sample is shown in Table D-4, page 87. The basic total of 296 respondents was reduced to 255 because of 41 respondents selected from the screening survey sample, who advised that their units did not practice management science as defined in the study. All answers from these 41 respondents were deleted from the data set prior to tabulation and are not reflected in the study.

Table D-2: Sample Design, Responses and Response Rates for Screening Phase of Study

	Sample Selected	Number Responding	Response Rate[1]
Size of Company			
Large - over 50,000 employees	69	41	59%
Medium - 10,000 to 49,999	352	139	39
Small - 500 to 9,999[2]	833	312	37
Total	1,254	492	39%
Type of Business			
Nonmanufacturing	38	23	60
Manufacturing	714	281	39
Industrial Average	752	304	40%
Transportation/Utility	109	69	65
Trade/Service	142	40	28
Financial	251	77	31
Service Average	502	186	37%
Company Headquarters Location (Census Region)			
Northeast	467	155	33
North Central	420	177	42
South	238	95	40
West	129	63	49

[1] Response rates for individual size classes ranged from a high of over 68 percent for the largest class (over 100,000 employees) to a low of 14 percent for the smallest size class (0 to 249).

[2] The combined effects of low initial probability of selection, low response rates, and low MS/OR incidence reduce the proportion of respondents in companies having fewer than 500 employees to less than 1 percent; the small size class, therefore, effectively refers to companies having 500 - 9,999 employees in the substantive data.

Table D-3: Incidence of Management Science/Operations Research Units, Screening Survey Data*

	Have MS/OR Unit(s)	No MS/OR Unit	MS/OR Incidence Rates $\frac{a}{(a+b)}$ 100	Adjusted MS/OR Incidence Rates[1]
	(a)	(b)		
Size of Company				
Large	28	13	68%	61%
Medium	73	66	53	45
Small	103	209	33	30
Type of Business				
Nonmanufacturing	12	11	52	46
Manufacturing	130	151	46	40
Industrial Average	142	162	47	40%
Transportation/Utility	20	49	29	24
Trade/Service	12	28	30	23
Financial	30	47	39	35
Service Average	62	124	33	29%
Census Region				
Northeast	70	85	45	40
North Central	76	101	43	36
South	28	67	29	25
West	30	33	48	41

* All data shown are unweighted. Totals, therefore, are omitted because of disproportionalities in both the sampling plan and the response rates. In addition, some classes of businesses in the universe were not sampled at all (e.g., consulting and professional service firms).

[1] Adjusted to correct for 41 unit managers who responded in the substantive survey that their units could not properly be considered MS/OR units. (See footnote 1, page 84.)

Table D-4:   Distribution of Respondents to Three-Part Substantive Survey

	Total Respondents		Actual Respondents[1]		Respondents Not Practicing MS/OR[1]	
	Number	Percent	Number	Percent	Number	Percent
Size of Company						
Large - 50,000 employees and over	53	18%	48	19%	5	12%
Medium - 10,000 to 49,999	143	48	127	50	16	39
Small - 500 to 9,999	100	34	80	31	20	49
Total	296	100%	255	100%	41	100%
Type of Business						
Nonmanufacturing	30	10	28	11	2	5
Manufacturing	175	59	149	58	26	63
Industrial Average	205	69%	177	69%	28	68%
Transportation/Utility	31	10	26	10	5	12
Trade/Service	21	7	17	7	4	10
Financial	3913	35	14	4	10	
Service Average	91	31%	78	31%	13	32%
Company Headquarters Location (Census Region)						
Northeast	93	31	81	32	12	29
North Central	111	38	94	37	17	41
South	49	17	43	17	6	15
West	43	14	37	14	6	15

[1] Only data from "actual" respondents used in study; data from Respondents Not Practicing MS/OR deleted prior to tabulating study tables.

Table D-5:   Distribution of Respondents by Questionnaires Answered

Respondents Answering	Questionnaire Number 1	Questionnaire Number 2	Questionnaire Number 3
All Three	131	131	131
Two out of Three	50	48	6
One out of Three	74	8	11
Total Responding	255	187	148

Selected Bibliography on Management Science/Operations Research

Books and Monographs

Ackoff, R. L. *A Concept of Corporate Planning.* New York: John Wiley & Sons, 1970.

————— , and Rivett, P. *The Manager's Guide to Operations Research.* New York: John Wiley & Sons, 1963.

Ansoff, H. Igor. *Corporate Strategy.* New York: McGraw-Hill Book Company, 1965.

Anthony, R. N.; Dearden, J.; and Vancil, R. F. *Management Control Systems,* rev. ed. Homewood, Ill. Richard D. Irwin, Inc., 1972.

————— . *Planning and Control Systems: A Framework for Analysis.* Cambridge, Mass.: Graduate School of Business, Harvard University, 1965.

Aronfsky, J. S. *Progress in Operations Research,* Volume III: "Relationship Between Operations Research and the Computer." New York: John Wiley & Sons, 1969.

Arrow, Kenneth J.; Karlin, Samuel; and Scarf, Herbert. *Studies in the Mathematical Theory of Inventory and Production.* Stanford, Cal.: Stanford University Press, 1958.

Baumol, William J. *Economic Theory and Operations Analysis.* Englewood Cliffs, N.J.: Prentice-Hall, Inc., 1961.

Beer, Stafford. *Management Science: The Business Use of Operations Research.* Garden City, N. Y.: Doubleday & Company, 1968.

Bierman, Harold, Jr.; Fouraker, Lawrence E.; and Jaedicke, Robert K. *Quantitative Analysis for Business Decisions.* Homewood, Ill.: Richard D. Irwin, Inc., 1965.

Boettinger, Henry A. *Corporate Planning & the Management Sciences.* London: British Institute of Management, 1970.

Chernoff, Herman, and Moses, Lincoln E. *Elementary Decision Theory.* New York: John Wiley & Sons, 1959.

Churchman, C. West. *The Systems Approach.* New York: Dell Publishing Co., Inc., 1969.

—————; Ackoff, Russell L.; and Arnoff, E. Leonard. *Introduction to Operations Research.* New York: John Wiley & Sons, 1957.

Clark, William A., and Sexton, Donald E., Jr. *Marketing and Management Science: A Synergism.* Homewood, Ill.: Richard D. Irwin, Inc., 1970.

Cleland, David I. and King, William R. *Systems Analysis and Project Management,* New York: McGraw-Hill Book Company, 1968.

Cyert, Richard, and March, James G. *Behavioral Theory of the Firm.* Englewood Cliffs, N.J.: Prentice-Hall, Inc., 1963.

Day, Ralph L., ed. *Marketing Models: Quantitative and Behavioral.* Scranton: International Textbook Company, 1964.

Dean, Joel. *Managerial Economics.* Englewood Cliffs, N.J.: Prentice-Hall, Inc., 1951.

DeMasi, Ronald J. *An Introduction to Business Systems Analysis.* Reading, Mass.: Addison-Wesley Publishing Company, Inc. 1969.

Dorfman, Robert; Samuelson, Paul A.; and Solow, Robert M. *Linear Programming and Economic Analysis.* New York: McGraw-Hill Book Company, 1958.

Emery, James C. *Organizational Planning and Control Systems: Theory and Technology.* New York: The Macmillan Company, 1969.

Glans, Thomas B.; Holstein, David; Meyers, William E.; Schmidt, Richard N.; and Grad, Burton. *Management Systems,* New York: Holt, Rinehart & Winston, Inc., 1968.

Gordon, Geoffrey. *Systems Simulation.* Englewood Cliffs, N.J.: Prentice-Hall, Inc., 1969.

Greenwood, William T., ed. *Decision Theory and Information Systems.* Cincinnati: South-Western Publishing Company, 1969.

Hanssmann, Fred. *Operations Research Techniques for Capital Investments.* New York: John Wiley & Sons, 1968.

Hertz, David Bendel. *Does Management Science Provide Management Information?* Special paper for The Society for Management Systems, September, 1970.

_____ . *New Power for Management: Computer Systems and Management Science.* New York: McGraw-Hill Book Company, 1969.

Hillier, Frederick S., and Lieberman, Gerald J. *Operations Research.* San Francisco: Holden-Day, second edition, 1974.

Koopmans, Tjalling C., ed. *Activity Analysis of Production and Allocation.* New York: John Wiley & Sons, 1951.

Luce, R. Duncan, and Raiffa, Howard. *Games and Decisions.* New York: John Wiley & Sons, 1957.

March, James G., and Simon, Herbert A. *Organizations.* New York: John Wiley & Sons, 1958.

McCloskey, Joseph F., and Trefethen, Florence N. *Operations Research for Management.* Baltimore: Johns Hopkins Press, 1954.

McDonough, Adrian M. *Information Economics and Management Systems.* New York: McGraw-Hill Book Company, 1963.

Meier, R. C., Newell, W. T., and Pazer, H. L. *Simulation in Business and Economics.* Englewood Cliffs, N.J.: Prentice-Hall, Inc., 1969.

Miller, David W., and Starr, Martin K. *Executive Decisions and Operations Research.* Englewood Cliffs, N.J.: Prentice-Hall, Inc., 1960.

Mills, Harlan D. *Mathematics and the Managerial Imagination.* Princeton: Mathematica, 1959.

Moder, J. J., and Elmaghraby, S. E., eds. *Handbook of Operations Research,* New York: Van Nostrand Reinhold, forthcoming.

Montgomery, David B., and Urban, Glen L. eds. *Applications of Management Science in Marketing.* Englewood Cliffs, N.J.: Prentice-Hall, Inc., 1970.

_____ . *Management Science in Marketing.* Englewood Cliffs, N.J.: Prentice-Hall, Inc., 1969.

Naylor, Thomas H.; Balintty, Joseph L.; Burdick, Donald S.; and Chu, Kong, *Computer Simulation Techniques*. New York: John Wiley & Sons, 1966.

PoKempner, Stanley J. *Information Systems for Sales and Marketing Management*. New York: The Conference Board, 1973.

——— , ed. *Decision Making in Marketing*. New York: The Conference Board, 1971.

Raiffa, Howard. *Decision Analysis*. Reading, Mass.: Addison-Wesley Publishing Company, Inc., 1968.

——— , and Schlaifer, Robert O., *Applied Statistical Decision Theory*. Boston: Harvard Business, 1961.

Rapoport, Anatol. *Fights, Games, and Debates*. Ann Arbor, Mich.: University of Michigan Press, 1960.

Rappaport, Alfred. *Information for Decision Making: Quantitative and Behavioral Dimensions*. Englewood Cliffs, N.J.: Prentice-Hall, Inc., 1970.

Richmond, Samuel B. *Operations Research for Management Decisions*. New York: Ronald Press, 1968.

Schlaifer, Robert O. *Introduction to Statistics for Business Decisions*. New York: McGraw-Hill Book Company, 1961.

——— . *Probability and Statistics for Business Decisions*. New York: McGraw-Hill Book Company, 1959.

Schuchman, Abe. *Scientific Decision Making in Business*. New York: Holt, Rinehart & Winston, 1963.

Shubik, Martin. *Game Theory and Related Approaches to Social Behavior*. New York: John Wiley & Sons, 1964.

Simon, Herbert A. *The New Science of Management Decision*. New York: Harper & Row, 1960.

——— . *Administrative Behavior*. New York: The Macmillan Company, 1947.

Starr, Martin. *Management: A Modern Approach*. New York: Harcourt Brace Jovanovich, Inc., 1971.

Thiel, Henri. *Economics and Information Theory*. Amsterdam, The Netherlands: North-Holland (distributed by Rand-McNally and Co., Chicago), 1967.

Vassonyi, Andrew. *Scientific Programming in Business and Industry*. New York: John Wiley & Sons, 1958.

von Neumann, John, and Morgenstern, Oskar. *Theory of Games and Economic Behavior*. Princeton, N.J.: Princeton University Press, third edition, revised, 1953.

Wagner, Harvey, *Principles of Operations Research with Applications to Managerial Decisions*, Englewood Cliffs, N.J.: Prentice-Hall, Inc., 1969.

Wald, Abraham. *Statistical Decision Functions*. New York: John Wiley & Sons, 1960.

——— . *Sequential Analysis*. New York: John Wiley & Sons, 1947.

Whitin, Thomson M. *The Theory of Inventory Management*. Princeton, N.J.: Princeton University Press, 1953.

Woolsey, Robert E. D., and Swanson, Huntington S. *Operations Research for Immediate Application: A Quick and Dirty Manual*. New York: Harper & Row, 1975.

Articles

Archer, Stephen H. "The Structure of Management Decision Theory." *Journal of the Academy of Management,* December, 1964.

Arrow, Kenneth J. "Utilities, Attitudes, Choice: A Review Article." *Econometrica,* January, 1958.

Bates, James. "A Model for the Science of Decision." *Philosophy of Science,* No. 21, 1954.

Boulding, Kenneth Ewart. "General Systems Theory: The Skeleton of Science." *Management Science,* April, 1956.

Greenwood, D. C. "Decision Trees and Decisions." *Production Engineer,* April, 1963.

Gorry, G. Anthony, and Scott Morton, Michael S. "A Framework for Management Information Systems." *Sloan Management Review,* Fall, 1971.

Levitt, Harold J., "Beyond the Analytical Manager" Spring and Summer issues, *California Management Review,* 1975.

Lundberg, Craig C. "Administrative Decisions: A Science for Analysis." *Journal of the Academy of Management,* Vol. 5, No. 2, 1962.

Marschak, Jacob. "Elements for a Theory of Teams." *Management Science,* January, 1955.

———— . "Economics of Inquiring, Communicating, Deciding." *American Economic Review,* May, 1968.

———— . "Economics of Information Systems." *Journal of American Statistical Association,* March, 1971.

PoKempner, Stanley J. "Is There a Management Scientist in the House?" *The Conference Board RECORD,* May, 1974.

Shubik, Martin. "Approaches to the Study of Decision Making Relevant to the Firm." *Journal of Business,* April, 1961.

———— . "Studies in Theories of Decision Making." *Administrative Science Quarterly,* December, 1958.

Simon, Herbert A. "Theories of Decision Making in Economics and Behavioral Science." *American Economics Review,* June, 1959.